AACRAO®

ACADEMIC DISHONESTY

Developing and Implementing Institutional Policy

by Dennis Bricault, Ph.D
North Park University

American Association of Collegiate
Registrars and Admissions Officers
One Dupont Circle, NW, Suite 520
Washington, DC 20036-1135

Tel: (202) 293-9161 | Fax: (202) 872-8857 | www.aacrao.org

For a complete listing of AACRAO publications, visit www.aacrao.org/publications/.

The American Association of Collegiate Registrars and Admissions Officers, founded
in 1910, is a nonprofit, voluntary, professional association of more than 10,000 higher
education administrators who represent more than 2,500 institutions and agencies in
the United States and in twenty-eight countries around the world. The mission of the
Association is to provide leadership in policy initiation, interpretation, and imple-
mentation in the global educational community. This is accomplished through the
identification and promotion of standards and best practices in enrollment management, information technology, instructional management, and student services.

LIBRARY OF CONGRESS CATALOGING-IN-PUBLICATION DATA

Bricault, Dennis.
Academic dishonesty / by Dennis Bricault.
    p. cm.
Includes bibliographical references.

ISBN 1-57858-080-3

1. Cheating (Education)—United States.
2. College students—United States—Conduct of life.
3. Students—Legal status, laws, etc.—United States.

I. Title.

LB3609.B73 2007
378.1'98—DC22
2007017694

Contents

Acknowledgments

I would like to thank Terry Williams, Associate Professor of Higher Education, Loyola University Chicago, whose guidance and encouragement on my initial research led to the publication of this booklet. My colleague at North Park University, Professor David Koeller, graciously allowed me to use his course syllabus and statement on academic honesty as a model for thoroughness. Finally, I am most grateful to the entire publications and editorial staff at AACRAO—Paula McArdle, Martha Henebry, and Amy Haavik—for their attentiveness and attention to detail at every stage of production of this booklet.

Dennis Bricault, Ph.D
Associate Professor of Spanish/Director, ESL Program
North Park University, Chicago, IL

Abstract

Academic dishonesty poses a threat to the goals of every educational institution. Drawing heavily from current literature, case law, and a survey of fifty-two North Park University faculty, I will provide an overview of academic dishonesty, paying particular attention to associated legal aspects. I will first define the types and range of academic dishonesty and examine the causes and manifestations of dishonest behavior. I will then analyze the legal issues affecting academic misconduct: case law, due process, the content and communication of policies, sanctions, prevention, and detection. The next section of the guide is a short risk evaluation of North Park's responses—individual as well as institutional—to instances of academic dishonesty. The final chapter offers a series of questions that are meant to guide administrators and faculty in informing or assessing the effectiveness of the procedures and policies in place at their institutions.

Introduction

"This is superior work," wrote a professor on a student's paper. *"It was excellent when Saint Thomas Aquinas wrote it, just as it is today. Saint Thomas gets an A. You get an F"* (Alschuler and Blimling 1995, p. 123).

Academic dishonesty is of great concern to educators, administrators, and students alike. On the surface, it appears to be a straightforward problem of outlining and enforcing a strict code of honor: faculty delineate the parameters of acceptable behavior, communicate these policies to the students, expect students to adhere to the guidelines, and enforce penalties for various types of infractions.

When administrators start to delve into the legal aspects of academic dishonesty, the once-clear waters suddenly become murkier. To begin with, universal agreement over what constitutes academic dishonesty does not exist: what some call cheating, others call collaboration. Next, policies are not always clearly written or well communicated. In addition, faculty are faced with the difficult decision of whether to handle instances of cheating on their own—a well-worn path—or to follow stated procedures and refer the student to a disciplinary committee—full of twists, turns, and bumps, the road less traveled. Finally, in an increasingly litigious society, faculty and administrators must be very careful to provide students with minimal due process so as to protect their rights.

This guide provides an overview of the forms, scope, and causes of academic misconduct, as well as the key legal bases that inform institutional procedures dealing with cases of academic dishonesty; the goal is to make faculty and administrators aware of due process and the need to communicate policies in a timely and consistent manner. Drawing from a wide range of literature as well as a survey of fifty-two faculty members at North Park University in Chicago, I will first describe the various forms of academic dishonesty and examine its scope on college campuses. Second, I will summarize the causes of cheating and the techniques used by dishonest students. In the third part of this study, I will delve into procedural and legal aspects of institutional regulations: legal bases, due process, communication of policy, and the types of sanctions imposed or suggested. I will then conduct a pilot risk assessment of North Park's policies and procedures used when addressing instances of academic dishonesty. I will close with an assessment plan, a series of questions meant to guide administrators and faculty in informing or assessing the effectiveness of the procedures and policies in place at their institutions.

◇◇◇◇◇◇◇◇◇◇◇◇◇◇◇◇◇◇

CHAPTER ONE

Defining the Problem

Trying to provide a succinct definition of academic dishonesty is a challenge, given its many facets. Some educators rely on legal or dictionary definitions; others fall back on metaphors and analogies. I would like to examine the various forms of misconduct, which will lead to a composite definition of academic dishonesty.

When dishonesty in the classroom is discussed, most teachers and students think first of cheating, "a fraud committed by deception; a trick, imposition, or imposture" ("The New Webster" 1971, p. 140). Cheating has been aptly termed "the academic equivalent of urban crime" (Alschuler and Blimling 1995, 123) and encompasses a laundry list of unacceptable behavior, such as "copying or attempting to copy from another student's work, [or] using or attempting to use unauthorized information, notes, [and] study aids" (Oakton Community College 1997, p. 21).

A second form of academic dishonesty is plagiarism, "an act of literary fraud in which one writer sets forth the words or ideas of another writer as his or her own in order to get gain" (Hatch 1992, p. 11). Whereas cheating is compared to stealing, plagiarism has been likened to forgery (Hatch 1992) or copyright violation (Maddox 1995), both more serious crimes: "among scholars, plagiarism is the worst of bad behavior...[and] is also the most tangible of academic misdemeanors" (Maddox 1995, p. 721). That said, plagiarism is more easily defined than it is universally recognized. Students are not always able to differentiate between plagiarism and correct paraphrasing (Roig

1997). The same holds true for faculty: Julliard (1994) found that English and medical faculty could not agree on what constituted plagiarism or how serious the alleged infractions were. This is but the first of many gray areas in the battle to provide a clear picture of what constitutes academic dishonesty.

Submitting another's work as one's own is a third form of academic misconduct. This ranges from simple cheating—copying another student's homework and turning it in—to outright fraud and counterfeiting, such as buying an essay or research paper from a term paper mill. This problem has mushroomed with the advent of the Internet—"a slacker's paradise of free computer games, pornography, and term papers" (Applebome 1997, p. 1)— and has extended beyond downloading entire term papers (McCollum 1996) to include buying and selling admissions essays (McCollum 1997).

Another form of academic dishonesty is the act of misrepresentation, fabrication or falsification of results (Dames 2006; Hatch 1992; Maddox 1995; Roig and Caso 2005), for example, "fudging" numbers on laboratory reports for a chemistry class (Deal 1984) or concocting an entire interview for a journalism assignment (Wolper 1997). Other kinds of academic fraud include, but are not limited to, "overstating credentials, exaggerating claims, withholding data, [and] misrepresenting facts or opinions" (Hatch 1992, p. 12).

Perhaps the most recent form of academic dishonesty revolves around the misuse of technology, particularly the Internet (Applebome 1997; McCollum 1996; Ross 2005), which makes it temptingly easy for students to plagiarize papers by cutting-and-pasting passages from web pages (Hansen 2003; Malesic 2006; Ross 2005; Smith, Dupre, and Mackey 2005). Misuse of technology is moving into the classroom in the form of cell phones equipped with cameras and text-messaging capabilities (Van Sack 2004).

In short, academic dishonesty can be viewed as a set of deliberate, unacceptable behaviors that students use to gain an unfair advantage on tests and assignments (Definitions 2006; Nelson 1995)—"plagiarism, cheating, ... alteration of institutional records" (Kaplin and Lee 1995, p. 457) and misrepresentation—or as a series of white-collar crimes—theft, forgery, and counterfeiting. Its seriousness cannot be underestimated, as it "runs counter to the goals and ideals of every educational institution and will not be tolerated...

and may result in dismissal" (North Park University 1997, p. 52) from a college or university.

As alluded to earlier, academic misconduct is not without its gray areas. Halfond (1991) provides a hypothetical case of a graduate business student who consults with a classmate about a take-home case-analysis exam. The student claims that the professor did not clarify her policy on collaboration, a particularly persuasive defense given the fact that many other class assignments were collaborative in nature. This begs the question of where collaboration ends and where cheating begins. Throughout this guide I will highlight disagreements among educators—particularly among North Park faculty—over the seriousness of some academically "dishonest" acts.

CHAPTER TWO

◇◇◇◇◇◇◇◇◇◇◇◇◇◇◇◇◇◇◇◇◇◇

Scope and Key Players

"There is no correlation between success and cheating; cheaters do not perform better on exams" (Dowd 1992, p. 9).

The literature is rich with studies and journal articles on academic dishonesty of all types; there have even been studies of studies, such as the exceptional summary in chart form of nineteen studies of misconduct and associated factors offered by Payne and Nantz (1994). As a means of providing an overview of the scope of academic dishonesty, I will synthesize the literature into two broad groups, general studies and variable-specific studies.

There have been several general studies that examine the prevalence of cheating on many campuses. In his ambitious 1964 project involving 5,000 students at 99 institutions, Bowers reported that 75 percent of the participants had cheated in some way at least once. McCabe and Trevino (1993) found a somewhat lower (but no less disturbing) rate of 67 percent among 6,097 students at 31 highly selective institutions. In a third study, May and Loyd (1993) reported academic misconduct rates of 40 percent to 60 percent.

Cheating activity has also been examined from a historical perspective. Steven Davis (1993) provided an excellent summary of numerous studies arranged by decade. In his synthesis, he underscored that the level of self-reported cheating rose from 23 percent in the 1940s to 38 percent in the 1950s, 49–64 percent in the 1960s, and 76 percent in the 1970s. McCabe and Trevino (1996) reported a notable increase in academic dishonesty—particularly during examinations—between 1963 and 1993. While more recent studies (Birchard 2006; McCabe, Butterfield, and Trevino 2006) confirmed such increases in instances of academic misconduct, Spiller and Crown (1995) attempted to control for types of cheating behavior over time (thereby neutralizing the effect of the different methodologies) and found no significant linear trend since the early 1900s.

The vast majority of studies on academic dishonesty have focused on specific variables associated with academic misconduct. Gender is one factor: women cheat less than men (S. Davis 1993; McCabe and Bowers 1996; Ward and Beck 1990), although this number is on the rise, particularly as women enter traditionally male-dominated majors (McCabe and Trevino 1993).

Personality traits form a second predictor of dishonest conduct: Weiss, Gilbert, Giordano, and Davis (1993) found a positive correlation between Type A personality, grade orientation, and high levels of academic dishonesty; Corcoran and Rotter (1987) positively associated self-punitive attitudes with the likelihood to cheat; and Ward (1986) recorded a positive correlation between self-esteem and honesty in classroom cheating situations.

Work habits comprise a third group of variables associated with academic dishonesty. Studies include Eisenberger and Shank's (1985) examination of the inverse relationship between a high work ethic and cheating and Roig and de Tommaso's (1995) report of a positive correlation between academic dishonesty and procrastination. Academic success—or the lack thereof—is another predictor in this category: "students with GPAs under 4.0 [on a 5.0 scale] are more likely to cheat" (Lipson and McGavern 1993, p. 16).

A fourth set of variables can be classified as "perceptions of and responses to" academic dishonesty. Ward and Beck (1990) discussed neutralization theory, a way to rationalize cheating by making "excuses...that help deflect commitments to conventional norms" (p. 334). Lipson and McGavern (1993) found that, even though academic dishonesty is on the rise at the Massachusetts Institute of Technology [MIT], "many of the students did not think what they had done was wrong" (1). Payne and Nantz (1994) examined student cultures that perceive academic dishonesty as more acceptable or less serious (as opposed to "blatant") and identified several "social accounts" used in defense of cheating. Thompson and Williams (1995) described the particularly sensitive issue of cheating by international students, who often have a vastly different view of what plagiarism and cheating entail. Foreign scholars may feel that freely copying a large excerpt of a text (without proper attribution) may show respect to the scholar and demonstrate the student's intelligence and good judgment in selecting sources.

A major branch of research on academic dishonesty targets institutional types and courses of study. Steven Davis (1993) found cheating to be more prevalent in high school than in college and more common at large institutions—public or private—than at small liberal arts colleges. Business students self-report the highest level of cheating among graduate professional students, with 76 percent of over six thousand respondents admitting that they had cheated in some way. English (71%) and medicine (68%) were close behind, while education (57%), law (63%), and the arts (64%) had the lowest levels of self-reported academically dishonest behavior (Tetzeli 1991). The problem is prevalent in graduate and professional schools as well: up to 58 percent of medical students self-report various types of cheating behavior (Rozance 1991, p. 2453), citing tremendous stress (Pellegrino 1991, p. 2454). Likewise, a 1998 survey (Beemsterboer, Odom, Pate, and Haden 2000) of forty-six dental schools found that an alarmingly high 91 percent of the schools reported between one and eight cases of academic misconduct over a two-year period.

Academic misconduct also occurs even before a student sets foot on a college campus. In addition to evaluating the merits of student applications, admissions staff must also scrutinize the applications for evidence of fraud. In addition to the previously mentioned online market for admissions essays (McCollum 1997), other forms of academic dishonesty related to the admissions process include transcripts that are counterfeit (Ferguson and York 2003; "Forged Transcripts" 2006; Lefkos 2006) or tampered with (Mangan 2002b); diplomas that have been purchased online (Foster 2003); fake letters of recommendation (De Francesco 2002; Mangan 2002a); and fraudulent scores on standardized tests (De Francesco 2002; Havers 1996).

◇◇◇◇◇◇◇◇◇◇◇◇◇◇◇◇◇◇◇◇

CHAPTER THREE

Causes and Manifestations

My favorite plagiarist, as I look back on a long career of teaching, was a freshman in my class at a highly selective Eastern woman's [sic] college, an institution that boasted of a strict honor code...I discovered that every paper she had given me...had been plagiarized. She knew it was wrong, she said with no embarrassment when I confronted her, but added she had no choice. Every weekend, when she should have been writing her papers, she was obliged, as national winner of the American Legion "Americanism" award, to give talks on American values at high schools all over the country. So she had no time to do her own work (White 1993, p. A44).

Having examined the scope of cheating (the "who"), I would like to turn my attention briefly to three other questions: the causes (the "why"), the opportunity (the "when"), and the most common techniques (the "how").

Causes

A few studies have focused on a broad view of the causes of academic dishonesty. Stevens and Stevens (1987) identified fourteen categories of reasons that students cheat, ranging from social pressure to personal values. Steven Davis (1993) and Lipson and McGavern (1993) cited stress, grades, time, workload, and course difficulty as among reasons that students cheat. In their study of "social accounts," Payne and Nantz (1994) listed peer pressure, a high rate of return (*i.e.*, less personal effort, low risk of getting caught, weak sanctions), and a value system that "do[es] not prohibit cheating" (p. 93). Other causes of cheating have been identified, such as unfair and/or overly demanding professors (McCabe and Trevino 1993), the fear of imminent failure ("Your Cheatin' Heart" 1992), and the belief that collaboration enhances the learning process (Lipson and McGavern 1993).

There are undoubtedly more reasons that students participate in academically dishonest behavior, but a shorter working list is sufficient to cover the majority of cases. McCabe and Trevino (1993) determined five main factors that influence academic dishonesty: peers' behavior, the existence of an honor code, the severity of penalties, the certainty of being reported, and the understanding of the institution's policy on academic integrity. The most strongly associated variable is peer behavior, which "may suggest that academic dishonesty not only is learned from observing behavior of peers, but that peers' behavior provides a kind of normative support for cheating" (McCabe and Trevino 1993, p.533). The authors found this especially true among women: as they compete with men in business and engineering classes, more are observing and imitating the behavior of their male counterparts.

A sixth factor should be added to this short list: ignorance. "Too many students stumble into plagiarism unawares, because they have never learned how to use sources properly, and sometimes even because they have been taught that research [in high school] means plagiarism" (White 1993, p. A44). In effect, honest students are apt to plagiarize by mistake rather than on purpose (Renard 2000). In a survey of fifty-two faculty members at North Park, one humanities professor observed that "most college students are just learning" to cite quotes and sources and would not consider such behavior dishonest. (See Figure 3.1 and Figure 3.2.) There is also a misunderstanding, particularly among international students, about who owns knowledge and thus what and whom to credit (Robinson 1992).

Opportunity
Academic misconduct can also be considered a crime of opportunity. Large classes and objective tests have always provided an inviting environment in which to copy during an examination. In contrast, the lack of clear institutional policies regarding academic dishonesty sends a mixed message to stu-

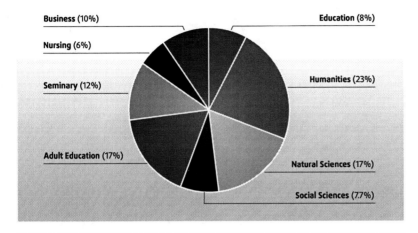

Figure 3.1: Respondents by Division/School

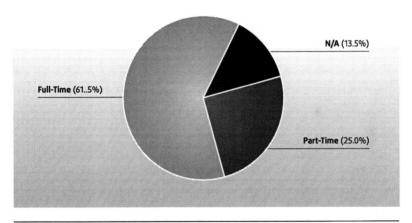

Figure 3.2: Faculty Status of Respondents

dents (S. Davis 1993; Lipson and McGavern 1993), particularly if they perceive that "everyone cheats" and gets away with it. Institutional culture may also promote misconduct: in one study, students at MIT believed that cheating was commonplace and admitted to collaborating on homework problem sets even when this activity was prohibited. They did not feel that either "cheating on exams or plagiarism...[was] an issue" (Lipson and McGavern 1993, p. 2).

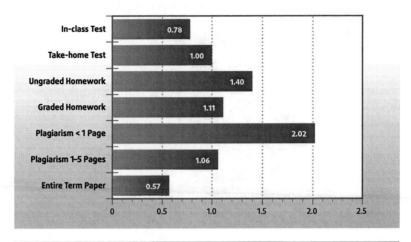

Figure 3.3: Frequency of Academic Dishonesty Encountered

Based on the results of the faculty survey, academic misconduct at North Park appears to be an occasional rather than a frequent occurrence. The lowest frequency among seven types of dishonest behavior is for plagiarizing an entire term paper, rated as "rarely" (0.57 on a scale of 0 to 5; with a low standard deviation of 0.72, suggesting strong agreement among the respondents; also relatively rare was cheating on an exam, either an in-class ($x = 0.78$, $\sigma_x = 0.83$) or take-home format ($x = 1.00$, $\sigma_x = 0.96$) (see Figure 3.3.). By far, the most common type of misconduct reported was plagiarism of less than a page, listed as "frequent" by seven respondents ($x = 2.02$, $\sigma_x = 1.42$).

Techniques

I hid a calculator down my pants...I had small velcro fasteners attached to my boots. I wrote the answers on paper that had velcro backs and attached them to my boots...[I put] notes in a plastic bag inside my mouth... I would make a paper flower, write notes on it, and then pin it on my blouse (S. Davis 1993, pp. 12–13).

As these four examples illustrate, some students will go to great lengths to gain an unfair advantage during a test. The list is as creative as it is long: Maramark and Maline (1993) listed a summary of twenty-six types of cheating activities mentioned in previous surveys, while Sutton and Huba (1995) identified fifteen techniques. Methods range from the run-of-the-mill copying from another student or using unauthorized crib notes to more brazen acts: stealing tests, using a proxy to take a test in one's place, telegraphing answers by using hand signals and tapping out codes, pre-programming a calculator with formulas, taping information in advance and listening to it on a walkman during the exam (S. Davis 1993), or using electronic receivers, pagers, or other devices (Croucher 1994; Fairclough 1995). Cell phones equipped with cameras loom as the next temptation for creative ways to cheat (Selingo 2004; "Students Using Cell Phones" 2005), though at some universities, the problem is not (yet) necessarily as prevalent as widely believed (Narita 2004). If the stakes are high, so are the costs involved: in a recent case, answers to standardized tests were inscribed on pencils and sold for between $2,000 and $9,000, depending on how high a score the student wished to achieve (Rogers 1996; Strosnider 1996; Weiser 1997).

Perhaps the most troubling development in recent years has been the growing number of Web sites that offer term papers on a wide variety of topics. Term paper mills have been around for years and typically charge $6–10 per page (Applebome 1997), more for customized papers, technical subjects, or express service (Witherspoon 1995). However, Internet sites are gaining a competitive edge by offering thousands of titles at a decidedly lower cost. Several Web sites with brazen names—"School Sucks," "Cheathouse," and "Other People's Papers"—offer free research papers to anyone who wants to download them. Many webmasters add thin disclaimers or defend themselves by contending that their sites are "not intended to promote plagiarism" (McCollum 1996, p. A28). They are quick to add that professors, too, can access the Web site to check the resources against papers that have been submitted, something which is not possible with mail-order term paper mills. Others make no bones about the purpose of the service by admitting "no problem with students' choosing to use the papers as their own" (Applebome 1997, p. 32). It remains to be seen how many students will make use of these Web sites and what impact such papers will have on higher education.

◇◇◇◇◇◇◇◇◇◇◇◇◇◇◇◇◇◇◇◇◇◇

CHAPTER FOUR

Legal Aspects

In the field of discipline, scholastic and behavioral, an institution may establish any standards reasonably relevant to the lawful missions, processes, and functions of the institution. It is not...unlawful...to prohibit the exercise of a right guaranteed by the Constitution or a law of the United States to a member of the academic community (District Court, Kansas City, MO 1968, p. 145).

Inasmuch as academic dishonesty undermines fundamental educational goals, an institution must set forth policies that discourage and penalize instances of misconduct. In this section, I will provide a summary of legal bases which inform policies on academic dishonesty, examine how such policies are communicated to students, describe due process in handling cases of misconduct, and discuss degrees of seriousness and corresponding sanctions. I will draw heavily from several sources of law as well as the survey of North Park faculty.

Legal Bases

When one begins to compile the sources of law upon which policies dealing with academic misconduct are premised, a number of dichotomies emerge. First is the classic categorization of public versus private control. Public institutions and their officers are subject not only to administrative rules and regulations, but also to a wide variety of external sources, such as state constitutions and/or statutes and the United States Constitution (Kaplin and Lee 1995). Private institutions such as North Park University are not bound by the U.S. Constitution; they are therefore relatively free from federal government control (*Trustees of Dartmouth College v. Woodward* 1819) and able to "formulate [their] own rules of conduct and impose these rules upon those students who enter the contract with [them]" (Weeks and Rice 1986, p. 4). This is not to suggest, however, that these institutions have carte blanche in their daily operations; they are subject to a number of federal statutes which prohibit discrimination based on factors such as race, sex, and age, although many independent colleges may use religion as a "bonafide occupational qualification" (Kaplin and Lee 1995, p. 199) to be exempt from the requirements of Title VII of the Civil Rights Act of 1964. In addition to federal statutes, private institutions rely heavily on contract theory (Weeks 1997), laws of professional associations (Weeks and Rice 1986), denominational guidelines, academic custom and usage, and internal rules and regulations (Kaplin and Lee 1995) as sources of law.

A second dichotomy that emerges in the arena of academic misconduct is the manner in which a case is handled—either according to a clearly stated procedure or in an arbitrary, capricious, or ambiguous manner. The key federal law in dealing with cases of misconduct is the Due Process Clause of the Fourteenth Amendment, which guarantees the accused party's right to hear and respond to charges made against him/her. The consequences of an institution's providing or failing to provide due process to the student has informed case law not only for public but also for private institutions. An early case that tested the Due Process Clause in higher education was *Dixon v. Alabama State Board of Education* (1961), which established the requirements of notice and a hearing as minimal safeguards for students accused of misconduct. The courts will consider a lawsuit if faculty or administrators are charged with acting in a capricious or arbitrary manner (*Board of Curators of University of Missouri v. Horowitz* 1978; *Carr v. St. John's University, New York* 1962; *Coscio v. Medical College of Wisconsin* 1987; *Milam and Marshall* 1987; *Regents of University of Michigan v. Ewing* 1985; *Shuffer v. Board of Trustees of the California State University and Colleges* 1977) or if the stated procedures are overly broad and vague (*Soglin v. Kauffman* 1969).

A third and final dichotomy is whether cheating and plagiarism should be treated as academic or social misconduct. This distinction has not always been clear to the courts, which view scholastic dishonesty as "an offense which cannot be neatly characterized as either 'academic' or 'disciplinary'" (*Jaska v. Regents of University of Michigan* 1984, p. 1248). When the infraction is considered academic, "by and large the American courts have been loathe to involve themselves..., accepting as a general rule non-interference in a university's purely academic decisions" (Dwyer and Hecht 1994, p. 7). As such, courts have generally deferred to an institution's academic judgment (Dwyer and Hecht 1994), illustrated by such landmark cases as *Woodruff v. Georgia State University* (1983), *Regents of University of Michigan v. Ewing* (1985), *Swidryk v. Saint Michael's Medical Center* (1985), and *Susan M. v. New York Law School* (1990) and upheld by more recent court decisions, such as *Blaine v. Savannah Country Day School* (1997). However, if the lawsuit moves away from the academic into the disciplinary arena, the courts are more willing to intervene. Even though such lawsuits involve fundamental constitutional rights—due process, property claims, or civil rights—not all of the constitutional safeguards afforded to criminal defendants are guaranteed to the cheaters (Dwyer and Hecht 1994; Swem 1987), such as the right to produce and/or cross-examine witnesses (*Reilly v. Daly* 1996). Likewise, contractual procedures and protections in institutional publications (*e.g.*, college catalogues and student handbooks) are enforceable, an especially important point for private institutions (*Zumbrun v. University of Southern California* 1972). No additional safeguards are guaranteed, however, if they are not stated, nor does the list of violations have to be all-inclusive (*Boehm v. University of Pennsylvania School of Veterinary Medicine* 1990).

Due Process

The courts have found that students enjoy the right to due process when faced with a potential loss of property or liberty rights (*Goss v. Lopez* 1975); this right is minimal rather than comprehensive (*Gaspar v. Bruton* 1975), provided that the institution follows its own stated procedures (*Melvin v. Union College* 1993; *Tedeschi v. Wagner College* 1980; *Woody v. Burns* 1966) and that these procedures are neither capricious nor arbitrary (see above). Professional associations also provide a legal point of reference by supporting basic procedural safeguards: Section VI of the 1993 "NASPA Statement on Student Rights and Freedoms" underscores the importance of clear standards of conduct, investigation of misconduct, and hearing procedures (pp. 11–16).

Students who are accused of academic dishonesty but are denied due process may prevail in a court of law (*Greenhill v. Bailey* 1975; Wagner 1993; *Weideman v. SUNY College at Cortland* 1992), especially when the sanctions are more serious (*i.e.*, ranging from suspension [*Esteban v. Central Missouri State College* 1967; *Goss v. Lopez* 1975] to expulsion [*Dixon v. Alabama State Board of Education* 1961; *Weideman v. SUNY College at Cortland* 1992]). Some courts have maintained due process requirements less stringently in cases of purely academic misconduct. However, an institution—public or private— that follows stated procedures will maintain a strong legal position (*Clayton v. Trustees of Princeton University* 1981; Dannells, 1997), particularly when the instances fall squarely on the academic side of the misconduct continuum.

"Probably the case that has set forth due process requirements in greatest detail" (Kaplin and Lee 1995, p. 486) is *Esteban v. Central Missouri State College* (1967), in which the courts established a number of safeguards for defendants in disciplinary hearings. Dwyer and Hecht (1994) summarized these due process requirements for bringing a student up on a charge of academic dishonesty in three basic legal steps: "timely notification of any accusation of misconduct, a timely hearing where the student may hear the accusations from the accuser(s) themselves, and an opportunity for the accused to present their [sic] side of the story" (p. 8). Also strongly suggested are the following additional steps: "written notice of the witnesses to appear against the student..., an opportunity to inspect evidence, and written findings of fact and basis for decision" ("Disciplinary Dismissals" 1986, p. 1).

Many, if not most (Jendrek 1989), faculty members choose to bypass existing procedures for dealing with academic dishonesty (Bell 2005) because they are "time-consuming and usually adversarial [and require] the difficult burden of proof" (Alschuler and Blimling 1995, p. 124). They feel that their authority is undermined because they "can give an F for lousy work, but not for alleged cheating" (p. 124). Risacher and Slonaker (1996) opposed using a failing grade as "punitive action against a student for behavior that violates an institution's academic misconduct policy" (pp. 115–116). Instead, they regarded academic misconduct as a behavioral issue *requiring* due process for the accused party. Kibler (1993a) noted that an "F" for academic misconduct is both ineffective and misleading: it does nothing to deter weak students from cheating, and it fails to give the student an opportunity to address the root causes of the dishonest behavior.

Stevens (1996) observed that there are rarely clear-cut procedures for dealing with minor instances of cheating. He brought up a number of issues to consider when a faculty member attempts to deal with academic dishonesty on his/her own rather than taking it through established channels: the level of seriousness, the severity of penalty, and the type of notice given (oral or written). He suggested that instructors follow what he terms the Supreme Court's "due process paradigm" (pp. 141–143) when handling a minor incident on one's own.

◆ **Preliminary Steps:** "The professor should take whatever time is necessary to develop a calm, rational approach" (p. 142) considering the seriousness of the incident and the level of sanction to be imposed.

◆ **Notice Procedure:** The instructor communicates the allegation to the student, asks for his/her response, and informs him/her of the appeal process.

◆ **Hearing Procedure:** "The amount of process due depends upon the entitlement or interest at stake," (p. 143) but need not include all the elements of a criminal trial, such as attorneys, witnesses, and oaths (Swem 1987). Likewise, the "burden of proof" borne by the accuser (*i.e.*, the faculty member) is relative to the severity of the infraction: minor instances of cheating need only show "simple preponderance of the evidence" (Stevens 1996, p. 143).

Content and Communication of Policies

Hoekema (1994) offered a three-prong test to determine the legitimacy of an institutional policy on student conduct. It should serve to "prevent or punish exploitation and harm inflicted or suffered by students; prevent or punish behavior that undermines the academic values of free discussion and learning; or foster a sense of moral community and mutual responsibility" (p. 134).

Clearly, policies on academic integrity must pass muster on the second and third tests and perhaps on the first as well. Because such policies protect free discussion, learning, moral community, and mutual responsibility, they should be clearly communicated to students early and often in their academic career.

Two studies provide opposing views of the presence of policies on academic integrity. In his survey of a mix of 183 public and private colleges and universities, Aaron (1992) found that 95 percent had an academic integrity code and 98 percent had procedures for dealing with instances of misconduct. A different perspective is offered by Steven Davis (1993), who found that "of 200 catalogs surveyed, only 55 percent contained" (p. 15) statements on academic dishonesty.

There are many methods for providing students with information about how the institution deals with academic dishonesty. The college catalog may include a statement on basic rules, regulations, and expectations. A department or school may provide its majors with informational booklets and web pages. However, the student handbook is the most common medium for communicating institutional policies on dealing with academic dishonesty, followed by the college catalogue and new student orientation (Aaron 1992). A comprehensive statement will include parameters of unacceptable behavior (definitions as well as examples) and a description of the disciplinary and appeal process; "at minimum the institution should describe realistically the mutual obligations of both the college and the student" (Weeks and Victor 1982, p. 2).

The student handbook is an internal source of law and is frequently viewed as a major component of the contract between the student and the institution. Accordingly, the handbook must be drafted with utmost care, because

> ...while the entire [student] handbook may not be construed as contractual in nature, courts have increasingly imputed contractual relationships. In certain critical areas, particularly those dealing with suspension and expulsion, the courts have said that colleges must follow their own procedures. (Weeks and Victor 1982, p. 1)

In addition, courts do not automatically extend all contract law theories to student handbooks due to the unique nature of the student-university relationship. As a generalization, however, the contractual relationship is present "especially when disciplinary matters are involved" (Weeks 1996, p. 3).

Even though all students may receive a student handbook, they may not read it carefully, if at all. Thus the role of the faculty assumes paramount importance in taking the lead on promoting academic integrity. Aaron (1992) noted the need to inform faculty of institutional policies on academic integrity; while accomplished primarily through the faculty handbook, some instructors are given student handbooks or are briefed on the topic during faculty orientation. McQuade (2007) recommended that professors be proactive in discussing with their students the temptations and dangers of engaging in "cybercrime" with the increasing array of technology at students' disposal.

The American Association of University Professors (AAUP) Ethics Statement (1994) charged the faculty with "maintaining honest academic conduct" (p. 2) in their classrooms through preventative measures such as written guidelines on the first day of class. As such, the course syllabus is another line of defense against academic dishonesty and must include information about both appropriate and inappropriate behavior as well as the consequences of engaging in cheating and plagiarism (Leeds 1992). In addition to the syllabus, Alschuler and Blimling (1995) stressed the importance of the faculty's frequent and clear communication of their expectations of academic honesty to students (Guiliano 2000) throughout the course: "at the beginning of class, before exams, prior to writing papers and doing lab work" (p. 125). Wilhoit (1994) suggested building into lesson plans a variety of activities that illustrate acceptable and unacceptable scholarship: discussing what constitutes plagiarism; examining hypothetical cases; reviewing conventions of citation and documentation; and requiring multiple drafts. Students therefore must make use of both formal and informal channels to be educated about the procedural and ethical issues involved in academic integrity (Pancrazio and Aloia 1992).

All students at North Park University receive (and must sign for) the "Student Handbook and Daily Planner" (1997) on registration day. Part three of the Handbook, entitled *All the Fine Print: A Resource for Policies, Rules, and Regulations* (pp. 47–74), includes a four-page section (pp. 52–55) on academic dishonesty (see Appendix C, on page 55). The section first breaks down five types of academic misconduct (with numerous examples of each type) and closes with procedures of due process: notice, involvement of the dean of the faculty, the hearing process, the appeal process, and a range of sanctions.

Most North Park faculty members prefer to take a proactive stance in communicating policies on academic integrity to students. Of the fifty-two faculty members surveyed, forty-six (88%) used at least one means of informing students of these policies, and twenty-six (50%) use two or more methods (see Figure 4.1). Thirty-two instructors chose to announce their policies sometime during the course, nineteen referred students to the student handbook, and fifteen included a statement in the course syllabus. Of the six professors who did not inform their students of the policies, most provided a reason:

◆ "I don't feel that it should need to be mentioned." (Natural Sciences/ Math Division)

◆ "I don't. It's included in our catalogue and teachers' handbook as it relates to college policy." (School of Education)

◆ "I assume they know dishonesty is forbidden. I don't spell out that [academic misconduct is] wrong and unacceptable." (Social Science Division)

◆ "I don't. I expect them to be awake and aware." (Natural Sciences/ Math Division)

In addition to the survey, I examined 177 course syllabi on file at the university library for statements on academic dishonesty. There were syllabi from nineteen of the forty-one undergraduate departments and from sixty-six different professors, so the sample should be considered representative. Business and psychology had the largest number of syllabi on file, with edu-

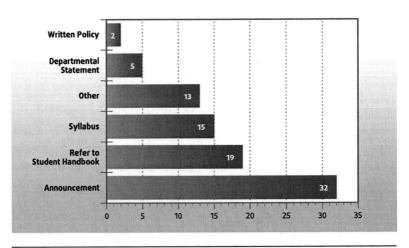

Figure 4.1: Methods Used for Communicating Policies on Academic Dishonesty

cation, history, biblical studies, foreign languages, and politics/government also well represented. I found that only twenty-four syllabi (14%) contained "comprehensive statements" on academic dishonesty (see Figure 4.2); this figure is misleading, since two professors accounted for half of these statements. Ten other syllabi (6%) referred students to other sources, such as the student handbook, and seven syllabi contained a very short observation, such as "Plagiarism will not be tolerated. You will find examples of good papers on reserve at the library." Other references ranged from boilerplate statements (*i.e.*, expected behavior, definitions, and penalties) to more ominous warnings: "Plagiarism will result in failure of the course" and "If I catch any students plagiarizing, I will expel them from the course, fail them in the course, report them to [the department chair] and all relevant deans, and do my best to have them expelled from the college."

Seriousness and Sanctions

"A weary slap on the wrist, such as a lowered grade on a paper, is the worst that practiced plagiarists expect if they happen to be caught" (White 1993, A44).

In a recent case of academic misconduct, two law students at St. Thomas University were found guilty of plagiarism but received a very light sanction:

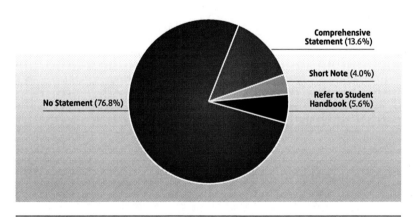

Figure 4.2: Reference to Policies on Academic Dishonesty in Course Syllabus

they each had to write a five-page paper on plagiarism. Even so, the students threatened to sue the school to keep their records clean (Mangan 1997). This case illustrates a central concern when dealing with academic dishonesty: the difficulty of ascribing a punishment that fits the crime. The accusers contend that harsh sanctions will act as a deterrent, while the accused argue that their rights are being violated by any penalty at all because "everyone cheats," and their only crime was that they got caught. In this section, I will look at the reactions of faculty when they encounter incidents of academic misconduct, their opinions over the severity of different types of dishonest behavior, and the range of sanctions suggested or imposed.

Private institutions enjoy particular latitude when enforcing penalties for misconduct, including a "jail sentence (failure of the course)" (Leeds 1992, p. 5), suspension (*Dehaan v. Brandeis University* 1957), and even expulsion (*Carr v. St. John's University, New York* 1962). More likely than not, instances of academic dishonesty are handled informally and do not even make the headlines in the college newspaper, let alone the national press. The irony of handling academic dishonesty on an informal, case-by-case basis is that the campus community is unaware of the actual level of cheating that occurs ("Hidden" 2005) and "may never be able to change the campus culture that causes it" (Alschuler and Blimling 1995, p. 123). As such, academic misconduct may be the best-kept secret on campus, particularly among senior administrators: Risacher and Slonaker (1996) submitted that as many as half of the 294 chief student affairs officers surveyed may be underestimating the degree to which students at their respective institutions engage in academic misconduct, though this may or may not be true among faculty (Hard, Conway, and Moran 2006).

Several studies have looked at how faculty deal—or fail to deal—with instances of misconduct. Inactivity is a common response: Lipson and McGavern (1993) found that faculty opt to do nothing 87 percent of the time because "cheating [is] difficult to prove" (p. 22). Verbal confrontation (such as warnings) with the offender is another technique (Dannells 1997; S. Davis 1993; Lipson and McGavern 1993). Faculty often choose not to formally charge the student because the institution's policy on academic dishonesty may actually hinder a unified faculty response to cheating if the procedures are too long or unclear (Dowd 1992; Lipson and McGavern 1993; McCabe

| *Academic Dishonesty*
Legal Aspects

2005; Selingo 2004). Even administrators recognize that faculty may not be familiar with existing formal channels for handling cases of misconduct: 62 percent believe that faculty tend to handle cases on their own "without utilizing established procedural guidelines" (Aaron and Georgia 1994, p. 85) and 41 percent think that "the majority of faculty are unaware of procedural guidelines for handling" (Aaron and Georgia 1994, p. 85) these cases.

Some institutions have attempted to address this "all-or-nothing" response to academic dishonesty. Rutgers University, for example, has developed a two-tiered system—based on the level of seriousness—for dealing with instances of academic dishonesty that has resulted in reducing multiple instances of cheating. Faculty can choose to handle less serious infractions on an individual basis. If the student agrees to this method (as opposed to a disciplinary hearing), sanctions are usually less severe, but a signed statement becomes part of the student's file; in addition, the student must enroll in a non-credit course on academic honesty. More serious instances of cheating are referred to a disciplinary hearing and may result in academic dismissal (Fishbein 1994).

As I alluded to earlier, faculty are not always of the same mind when asked what constitutes academic dishonesty, nor do they agree when queried about the seriousness of each type of misconduct. As part of my survey of fifty-two North Park faculty members, I asked respondents to rate seventeen types of behavior on a six-point Likert scale as "less serious" (0–1), "serious" (2–3), or "more serious" (4–5) (see Appendices A [page 47] and B [page 51]).

The types of behavior were grouped into three main clusters. In the first category, test-taking, faculty members rated "looking at books or notes" and "looking at another student's test" as the most serious forms of misconduct ($x = 4.25$, $\sigma_x = 1.03$, and $x = 4.12$, $\sigma_x = 0.96$, respectively). Although "having access to an earlier version of the test" and "glancing at another student's test" also were considered "serious," they also had high standard deviations ($\sigma_x = 1.63$ and $\sigma_x = 1.42$, respectively), suggesting a fair amount of disagreement among instructors, even within the same division, about the seriousness of each action. (See Figure 4.3, on page 26.)

In the second category, misconduct on homework assignments, one type of academic dishonesty stood out: "copying graded assignments," with a high average of 3.9 and low standard deviation of 1.14; "copying ungraded assignments" was also considered a serious offense (x = 2.92, σ_x = 1.38). Surprisingly, "consulting with another student" was rated as "less serious" (x = 1.42, σ_x = 1.34), which may be the result of a large number of collaborative out-of-class assignments. (See Figure 4.4.)

The third and final cluster is comprised of potentially dishonest behavior on major papers and projects. Here the faculty responded with a clear voice against "buying or downloading a term paper," with a rating of 4.79 (σ_x = 0.41). It appears from the data that failure to attribute sources properly is considered a particularly serious offense among North Park faculty. Certainly "failing to cite many quotes" rates as the most serious (x = 4.1, σ_x = 0.98), but even missing "one or two short quotes" is viewed as a serious infraction (x = 2.45, σ_x = 1.32). (See Figure 4.5.)

Having determined which actions the North Park faculty consider the most serious offenses, I asked them what sanctions they would impose (or had imposed in the previous instances).

There were two main sanctions suggested by about a third of the respondents. For dishonest behavior considered as "more serious" (assigned a rating of 4 or 5), the student would fail either the test/assignment (18 votes, or 36 percent) or the course (16 votes, or 32 percent). Another four instructors suggested failure of the course for repeat offenders. Other sanctions recommended were redoing the assignment, lowering the grade, placing the student

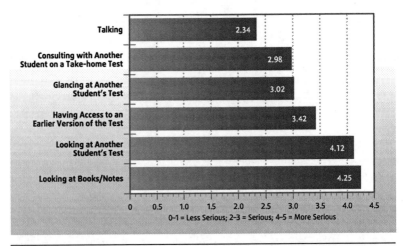

Figure 4.3: Degree of Seriousness of Dishonest Behavior during Test-Taking

Academic Dishonesty
Legal Aspects

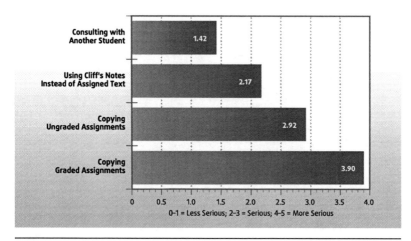

Figure 4.4: Degree of Seriousness of Dishonest
Behavior on Homework Assignments

on suspension or probation, and expelling the student. (See Figure 4.6, on page 28.)

It appears from the surveys that the vast majority of professors at North Park would opt to handle instances of academic dishonesty on their own. Only nine respondents mentioned outside entities (policies, handbooks, committees, the dean) for dealing with the most serious cases. It is therefore difficult to gauge the prevalence of academic dishonesty on campus (although

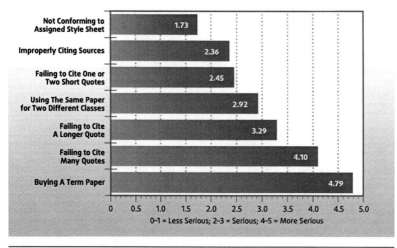

Figure 4.5: Degree of Seriousness of Dishonest
Behavior on Papers and Projects

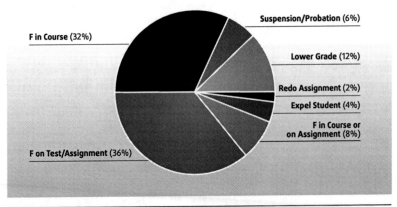

Figure 4.6: Suggested Penalties for "More Serious" Forms of Dishonest Behavior

the responses summarized in Figure 3.3 (on page 12) suggest that it is not a major problem), but faculty appear quite willing to fail students for what they consider the most serious offenses.

Prevention and Detection

"Unchecked acts of academic dishonesty injure the reputation of an institution, hurt students who earn grades through honest efforts, and render unlikely any positive learning on the part of the offenders" (Aaron and Georgia 1994, p. 90).

An overview of the topic of academic dishonesty would be considered incomplete without a brief foray into the areas of prevention and detection. I would like to examine campus-wide philosophies and several in-class methods of preventing and detecting misconduct.

There have been many approaches used to promote academic integrity. Perhaps the most recognizable tool is the student honor code system, which is widely believed to be an effective deterrent to academic dishonesty (May and Loyd 1993; McCabe and Bowers 1994; McCabe and Pavela 2005; McCabe and Trevino 1993; Turner and Beemsterboer 2003), although some authors (Jendrek 1992) do not fully share that view. Supporters of this system contend that a comprehensive institutional honor code can clearly spell out expectations and consequences as well as create an environment where academic honesty is respected (McCabe and Trevino 1996). Critics point out that, as institutions become larger and more culturally diverse, it will be increasingly difficult to develop and implement an honor code that all constituencies will accept and observe (McCabe and Trevino 1996).

"Our findings...suggest that the most important question to ask concerning academic dishonesty may be how an institution can create an environment where academic dishonesty is socially unacceptable" (McCabe and Trevino 1996, 30). What is needed, therefore, is cultural management—academic climate control, if you will—that will "promote and expect academic integrity and...help students develop the values needed to deal effectively with the moral and ethical dilemmas facing them" (Kibler 1994, p. 93). Such a shift will require support from key administrators and should feature significant student involvement (Alschuler and Blimling 1995). Many universities take a proactive approach by addressing issues of academic misconduct and honor codes during mandatory orientation, not only for incoming students (Academic Honesty Policy and Procedures 2004; How to Be Successful 2006; Plagiarism Information 2004), but for new faculty members as well (New Faculty Orientation 2006; New Student Orientation 2006). Some application forms even announce institutional policies regarding academic honesty to prospective students (Application for Admission 2007). These appear to be more common for applicants to graduate programs, however.

Recent research focuses on changing student attitudes toward campus misconduct, the so-called "student development" approach, which targets the demand rather than the supply side of the equation. It aims to foster a positive learning environment by emphasizing moral reasoning and behavior, clear policies, and opportunities for dialogue (Kibler 1993b). Proponents of this model argue that a concerted effort to "create a campus climate more conducive to academic integrity" (Fishbein 1994, p. 58) and "teach students how and why not to cheat" (Dowd 1992, p. 15) is more effective than an unwieldy system of sanctions and surveillance. Responses to instances of academic misconduct should be formative rather than punitive: faculty can "implement strategies that will help offending students understand the ethical consequences of their behavior" (McCabe 2005, p. 30). Furthermore, a punitive approach necessarily leads to an adversarial relationship between faculty and students, in which "faculty members are cast as 'policemen' or 'sheriffs' and students the sly little criminals they are out to thwart. Such an outlook immediately assumes that students have no morals or ethics and will cheat whenever they are given the opportunity" (Dwyer and Hecht 1994, p. 10).

The student development model has been elaborated to break this adversarial cycle. Payne and Nantz (1994) advocate a "comprehensive approach that emphasizes academic integrity policies, the dissemination of such policies to teachers and students, instructional precautions on exams and student assignments, and adherence to reporting and disciplinary procedures" (p. 94). Some proactive approaches that yield positive results include completing exercises on recognizing plagiarized passages (Landau, Druen, and Arcuri 2002), assigning specific topics for research papers and varying them each term, requiring multiple drafts (B. Davis, 1993; Sterngold 2004), and discussing assignments both in class and with individual students (Sterngold 2004). Kibler (1994) recommends a framework consisting of seven components for dealing with academic misconduct:

◆ An honor code
◆ Communication of policies
◆ Training of students, faculty, and teaching assistants about the nature of academic dishonesty, prevention techniques, effective testing procedures, handling violations, types of sanctions, and building academic integrity
◆ Faculty assistance
◆ Disciplinary procedures, highlighting due process and the role of sanctions
◆ Disciplinary process and programs, such as seminars and group sessions for violators
◆ Promotion of academic integrity
(pp. 93–94)

One campus constituency requires additional attention. In light of the increasing presence of international students on campuses across the country (Desruisseaux 1996), faculty will need to be trained in methods that will help foreign scholars overcome cultural misunderstandings about academically dishonest behavior. Suggested techniques (valuable not only to international students but also to their American classmates) include providing examples of proper citations and model papers; reading and discussing articles on cases of plagiarism and cheating; remembering to include cross-cultural examples; and practicing note taking, paraphrasing, summarizing, and using synonyms (Fanning 1992; Thompson and Williams 1995).

The best-laid plans of mice, men, administrators, and faculty will not deter every student from attempting to engage in dishonest behavior. As such, faculty will need several safeguards to protect themselves in the classroom against the most common forms of academic misconduct.

Cheating on in-class examinations has received the most attention from classroom researchers. There has been a long history of attempting to detect copying on objective tests by using statistical methods (Harpp 1991; Dwyer and Hecht 1994; Dwyer and Hecht 1996; Frary and Tideman 1997). At one institution, a computer program is used to compare the number of identical wrong answers given by students sitting near one another and to calculate the probability that this is due to chance; "cases of 3.5 million to one—or five standard deviations—are reported to the dean" (Harpp 1991).

Probabilistic methods may still not be enough to prove that two students copied. One pioneer cautions against the use of inferential statistics in identifying cheaters, saying, "a large number of identical errors on a single test item indicates that the item may be ambiguous or otherwise faulty and need revision or elimination" (Dickenson 1945, p. 541). Dwyer and Hecht (1996) submit that statistical tests should be used more for detection than prevention, and Frary and Tideman (1997) encourage the use of multiple methods for detecting and deterring cheating on tests.

Beyond statistical methods of detection, there are many suggestions for preventing cheating on tests. Hollinger and Lanza-Kaduce (1996) surveyed 1,672 students to measure potential deterrents of misconduct during exams. Among those rated by the students as most effective were scrambling tests, smaller classes, several proctors, unique make-up exams, multiple forms of the test, authorized use of study sheets during the exam, and more essay questions. Least likely to deter academic misconduct were more take-home exams and a "hotline" to report cheaters.

In contrast to spotting and deterring cheating on exams, detection and prevention of plagiarism is not as straightforward. Speaking from a student-development perspective, White (1993) observed that "students need to be taught how common ideas or ideas identified with particular writers can be made their own through their reflection upon them" (p. A44), best achieved in class by comparing examples of good and questionable citations and research (Fanning 1992; Thompson and Williams 1995; Wilhoit 1994). Specific suggestions designed to foil those who are considering term paper mills and Web sites include:

◆ Assigning more topics that require synthesis and analysis (as opposed to narration and description), such as comparing and contrasting two viewpoints
◆ Offering more specific topics (*e.g.*, "The Quaker Movement in the Midwest" rather than simply "The Quakers")
◆ Requiring multiple drafts of a paper

Students (as well as all researchers) can also avail themselves of a seven-step test advanced by Hatch (1992) to determine whether one author has plagiarized from another:

◆ "Is there a similarity between the two works?
◆ Did the writer have access to the other works?
◆ Is there evidence of copying?
◆ Is there a claim to originality?
◆ Is there an intent to deceive?
◆ Does the writer stand to gain anything by plagiarizing?
◆ Is there any copyright infringement?"
  (p. 12)

Institutions can promote academic integrity at all levels of campus life by means of an honor code or statement of ethics, early and frequent training in avoiding questionable behavior, communication and enforcement of policies, and in-class approaches to encouraging original and independent thinking.

Administrators and faculty need to be on the same page when considering academic dishonesty. There must be a comprehensive definition of the scope of unacceptable forms of misconduct, if one does not exist (McCabe 2005). It needs to be updated periodically, particularly in view of the rapid expansion of technology that can be misused in many ways. Campus leaders should be aware of the level of instances of academic dishonesty; faculty should be consistent in communicating their policies on, as well as presenting a consistent and fair response to, academic dishonesty.

◇◇◇◇◇◇◇◇◇◇◇◇◇◇◇◇◇◇◇◇◇

CHAPTER FIVE

Risk Evaluation

As a final step in my analysis of academic dishonesty, I would like to perform a brief risk evaluation of current practices at North Park University and identify potential legal issues that could emerge in the coming years.

The primary source of institutional policy on academic dishonesty is the "Student Handbook" (1997), reproduced in its entirety in Appendix C (on page 55). This four-page statement appears to contain all the basic pieces suggested by different sources throughout this guide: the goals of the policy, definitions and examples of five types of academic misconduct, a detailed outline of judicial procedures as well as the options that the student has at various stages of due process, a suggested range of sanctions, and a brief word on how the infraction will be recorded in the student's file. Because all students are required to sign for a new handbook every year, the University has provided itself with a legal defense: students have the most recent institutional policy in hand and are expected to be familiar with it.

The student handbook is but the first source of communication of institutional policies on academic dishonesty. All North Park faculty are required to provide students with a course syllabus during the first week of each term. In my study of 177 course syllabi on file at the library, I found that only 24 had a "comprehensive statement" on academic dishonesty. Table 5.1, on page 36, contains an analysis of selected statements from a legal perspective.

Statement	Analysis
#1 (from the Social Science Division)	
Ethics Code North Park University regards honesty and integrity as essential qualities in the practice and profession of management. Therefore, each student is expected to uphold and defend high ethical standards in the classroom and in all North Park activities. Each student is expected to promote and maintain an environment in which honor and trust complement and encourage a superior academic experience. In all academic activities at North Park, no student will: (a) give or receive unauthorized aid during completion of academic requirements; or (b) obtain, possess, or destroy property of another without consent; or (c) misrepresent fact or self at any time.	This statement contains two critical aspects described in the legal section of this guide: a purpose statement (the importance of ethical behavior) and broad examples of inappropriate behavior. What is lacking is the range of consequences of engaging in academic misconduct: will the student fail the exam, fail the course, or be referred to the Judicial Procedures Committee?
#2 (from the Humanities Division)	
Plagiarism is the unacknowledged use of another person's work, published or unpublished. 'Minor' instances will result in a failing grade on the assignment. Serious cases will result in failure of the course and possibly expulsion.	Although far less detailed than statement #1, this statement appears to do a more effective job of informing the student of the range of consequences that correspond to the seriousness of the infraction. The instructor will need to define what constitutes a "minor" instance of plagiarism.
#3 (from the Social Science Division)	
Any cases of plagiarism will be reported and forwarded to the dean's office. Please see the section "Academic Dishonesty" under the "Students' Rights and Responsibilities" in the current student handbook.	This statement is both concise and flexible, informing the student that misconduct is inappropriate and will be reported to an external body (although no word is given on the range of sanctions). The professor also places the responsibility squarely on the student for reading and understanding the institutional policy on academic dishonesty.
#4 (from the Humanities Division)	
Any form of plagiarism or dishonest examination behavior is unacceptable in this class or any other. Plagiarism is the unacknowledged use of another's ideas, language, or work for one's own gain. It is important to recognize, however, that one can commit plagiarism through unintentional carelessness as well as through deliberate theft. We will discuss plagiarism and how to avoid it. Remember: ignorance of the "law" is no excuse.	This statement takes a cue from the student development model by addressing unintentional plagiarism. The professor has agreed to take steps to teach students how to avoid plagiarism. There is no mention of possible sanctions in this statement; the professor must take care to discuss the range of penalties when he or she covers plagiarism in class.

Undoubtedly the most thorough statement on academic dishonesty in a North Park syllabus is provided by a history professor, David Koeller (see Appendix D, on page 59). The statement includes examples of both appropriate and inappropriate behavior, short definitions, and a range of sanctions. Of the twenty-five North Park syllabi available online, only Professor Koeller's contains any mention of academic integrity.

Because the syllabus is such an important document, one that is tailored to the parameters of each course, it is of paramount importance that North

Park faculty include a statement on expectations of academic integrity. As it stands right now, 76 percent of course syllabi (see Figure 4.2, on page 23) leave students in the dark, thereby opening up the potential escape valves of vagueness and lack of notice. A brief statement, such as #2 or #3 (see Table 5.1), will go a long way in avoiding future misunderstandings between students and instructors as to what constitutes academic misconduct and what sanctions may be imposed. Given the wide berth that faculty have in the grades they assign, the sanctions they suggest for serious offenses appear to be well within the legal boundaries discussed earlier in this section, provided they do not act in an arbitrary or capricious manner. Faculty who fail students for dishonest behavior must remember to inform students of the appeals process. The faculty may also wish to create a new failing grade to indicate that the student was failed due to academic dishonesty.

The North Park Student Handbook (see Appendix C, on page 55) provides a detailed account of due process available to students charged with academic misconduct. It includes all the elements suggested in Chapter Four (see "Due Process," on page 17):

◆ Initial notification of the alleged infraction by the faculty member
◆ Authorization of the initial decision by the faculty member (*i.e.*, the course instructor is given full authority to decide the sanction)
◆ Response by the dean of the university faculty, featuring notice to the student, an evaluation of the report filed by the faculty member, a meeting with the student to inform him/her of the right to appeal, and the record keeping requirement
◆ Options that the student has at that point
◆ The appeal process, including the composition of the judicial committee, the student's right to challenge committee members, and institutional policies on witnesses and type of forum (private)
◆ Range of actions that the judicial committee may take
◆ The student's right to appeal to the president of the university
◆ The range of sanctions

The Student Handbook distinguishes between due process for academic dishonesty and for disciplinary actions, with the latter providing a far more detailed breakdown of due process and sanctions.

It appears, therefore, that North Park's judicial procedures on academic dishonesty have been significantly shaped by case law and should face few, if any, legal challenges in the future. The institution will need to keep abreast of developments in challenges to sanctions, grades, and degrees awarded.

◇◇◇◇◇◇◇◇◇◇◇◇◇◇◇◇

CHAPTER SIX

Assessment Plan

Given the diversity of institutions of higher learning and the particular circumstances and characteristics of each college and university, it is very difficult to provide specific guidelines for the assessment of an institution's policies for dealing with instances of academic misconduct. Most likely, each institution has adequate procedures in effect; however, based on my own research and experiences at North Park University, I would like to offer a series of questions that can be used to inform or assess the procedures and policies in place at your own college or university. Wherever possible, I also offer illustrative examples from policies of various institutions around the country. Of course, any proposed plan or modification of the same should be run past legal counsel to ensure compliance with all existing legislation as well as congruency with institutional policies, practices, and customs.

Questions at the Institutional Level

EXISTENCE AND SCOPE OF POLICIES AND PRACTICES

◆ Does the institution have a comprehensive set of procedures for dealing with instances of academic misconduct?
◆ Are the procedures in accordance with existing legislation?
◆ Are the procedures congruent with the institution's mission, policies, customs, and/or existing honor code?

◆ Are there different (or potentially conflicting) policies and procedures for various schools, divisions, or programs on the same campus?

LOCUS AND COMMUNICATION

◆ Where can the policy be found? By way of example, Georgia College and State University (2007) notes that its statement on academic integrity is published in both the current catalog and in the student handbook.
◆ Who has access to the policy?
◆ Is the policy issued directly to faculty?
◆ Is the policy issued directly to students in some form (*e.g.*, in a student handbook)? The University of Maryland (2005), for example, refers to the honor code and the importance of academic integrity in every letter of acceptance sent by its admissions office.
◆ How does the institution ensure that students have seen, have been given, and/or have been informed of the policy? California State University, Fullerton (2003) clearly states in its online handbook that "the university expects students to know [the] rules [about appropriate academic conduct] and abide by them."

DUE PROCESS

◆ Do the procedures ensure the student's right to due process, including appeals?
◆ Are the procedures grounded in current legislation?
◆ How are students apprised of their right to due process? Wilmington College (2007) and the University of Rochester (2004) have put together useful sets of Web pages that focus on definitions, procedures, sanctions, and appeals.

REVIEW OF POLICIES AND PRACTICES

◆ When were the procedures most recently reviewed or even discussed? Cornell University's dean of the University Faculty, Charles Walcott, dedicated nearly a full page of his three-page 2004–2005 annual report to the Board of Trustees to the topic of academic integrity and the interest among faculty, students, and staff to discuss the issue of adopting an honor code.

◆ Who was involved in the review—*e.g.*, the governing board, administrators, faculty committee/senate, individual faculty members, representatives from student affairs, graduate and/or undergraduate students, the institution's legal counsel, etc.? In 1999–2000, Duke University (2007a) participated in a nationwide survey on the topic of academic dishonesty and found the need to reshape its procedures and develop a new honor code. Faculty, students, and administrators were brought into the process as the Academic Integrity Council (2007b).

COVERAGE

◆ How comprehensive are the procedures? There are numerous examples of institutional policies available online, but one that is noteworthy for its thoroughness is a twenty-five-page manual of policies and procedures developed by Syracuse University (2006b).

◆ Does the policy distinguish among and deal with specific types of academic misconduct? The State University of New York at Brockport (2003) has a detailed breakdown of types and recurrences of academic misconduct in its "Policy on Student Academic Dishonesty."

◆ Is it clear what range of sanctions and penalties are assessed for different types of infractions, and are these sanctions appropriate responses to the severity of each type of infraction? The Academic Honesty Policy adopted by the University of California, Merced (2007) provides a lengthy list of possible sanctions and distinguishes between those imposed by instructors and those enforced by formal disciplinary procedures.

PROCEDURES

◆ Are there distinct steps that clearly direct the parties involved; that is, do students, faculty, and administrators know who comes into play at each stage? Syracuse University (2006a) offers a flow chart to illustrate the procedures that instructors should follow in the event of alleged misconduct. The University of Florida (2007) has an "academic honesty process checklist" for faculty to follow when misconduct is suspected.

ACCEPTANCE BY CAMPUS ADMINISTRATORS

◆ Do key administrators—provosts, deans, department chairs, and student affairs officers—agree with the procedures as reasonable, workable, and effective? The preamble of George Washington University's (2005) "Code of Academic Integrity" begins with the words, "We, the Students, Faculty, Librarians, and Administration of The George Washington University, believing academic honesty to be central to the mission of the University, commit ourselves to its high standards and to the promotion of academic integrity."

ACCEPTANCE BY STUDENTS

◆ Have the policies and procedures been reviewed and approved by appropriate student representative groups (*e.g.*, student senate, student judicial board)?
◆ Do appropriate student leaders (*e.g.*, judicial board representatives, teaching assistants, tutors, resident directors) receive training in dealing with instances of academic misconduct?

OFFICIAL RECORDS

◆ Does the student transcript have special notations for failure of a course due to academic misconduct? Is this a permanent part of the student record, or does the institution have a grade forgiveness policy? These issues are addressed in the "Academic Integrity Policies" of Michigan Tech (2006) and Arizona State University (2007).
◆ Are these grading policies and procedures included in the overall institutional policy on academic dishonesty?

ELECTRONIC MEDIA

◆ Does the institution have a policy on the use of electronic devices (cell phones, listening devices, laptops, etc.) in classrooms? The policies and procedures at the State University of New York at Stony Brook (2006) contain a very specific list of such devices, general guidelines regarding their use (*e.g.*, during exams), and their potential for misuse.
◆ How is this policy enforced?

ORIENTATION

◆ Is part of new student orientation dedicated to issues surrounding academic misconduct (*e.g.*, plagiarism, cheating, appropriate and inappropriate uses of technology, and matters of using the internet in conducting research)? One session of new student orientation at the University of Pennsylvania (2006) features a skit performed by upper-class students "portraying situations relevant to life at Penn and a discussion about academic integrity policies."

Questions at the Faculty Level

COMMUNICATION

◆ How are faculty informed of the procedures for dealing with instances of academic dishonesty?
◆ Are new faculty members given an orientation to various issues associated with academic dishonesty? Topics may include the institution's definition or understanding of what constitutes academic misconduct, types of academic misconduct that are common on the campus, the initial steps in dealing with instances, the key campus personnel that need to be involved, the range of sanctions available, and a few dos and don'ts.

REVIEW OF POLICIES AND PRACTICES

◆ How often are the procedures reviewed with the faculty?
◆ Are faculty members apprised of changes in the procedures?
◆ When, where, and how does this happen?

ACCEPTANCE BY FACULTY

◆ Is there "faculty buy-in" of the procedures?
◆ Do the faculty feel that the procedures are reasonable, workable, and effective, or do they find them cumbersome and ineffective?
◆ How and how often are faculty members surveyed about the topic?

◆ Is there a standard policy statement about academic honesty that is required for inclusion in course syllabi (Spuches 2001)? If so, who monitors that this is being done? If not, should there be such a statement?

Questions at the Classroom Level

COMMUNICATION

◆ Does every instructor make some reference, either verbally or in writing, to his or her policy on academic misconduct? The University of Houston (2005) includes the following statement in its policy: "Faculty members are responsible for knowing the principles and procedures of the Academic Honesty Policy, and for enforcing it when academic honesty violations occur. Faculty members must also remind students of the Academic Policy and help them comply with it" (p. 3). Smith (2007) suggests issuing an "academic honesty contract" that students read, sign, date, and return to show that they have read and understood the class policies on academic misconduct and the possible consequences. The Office of Educational Development at the University of California, Berkeley (2006) suggests that faculty "remind students of any restrictions regarding the use of cell phones, pagers, palm pilots, and other similar devices in the classroom during exams" (p. 17).

PROACTIVE MEASURES

◆ At what point(s) in the student's academic career are issues of plagiarism and cheating addressed? For example, the first-year writing course at George Washington University (2007) "is designed to teach [students] to write and research responsibly and ethically" (p. 13).
◆ Do first-year writing courses discuss correct and incorrect forms of citation and the correct and incorrect use of web-based research? Florida State University (2004) builds a plagiarism exercise into the second week of its first-year writing course.
◆ Are examples of intentional and unintentional plagiarism provided? Yahn and Jordan (2007) developed an online activity for first-year writing stu-

dents at the University of Connecticut to help them distinguish between these two categories of plagiarism.

RESPONSES TO MISCONDUCT

◆ Does the instructor have an appropriate response to instances of misconduct?
◆ Is the response congruent with the student's right to due process?
◆ Is it in line with institutional policies and customs?

MULTI-LEVEL RESPONSES

◆ Is there a multi-tiered system of handling cases of academic misconduct? That is, do faculty members have the right to decide the appropriate response to "minor" instances of cheating or plagiarism on their own but can involve a campus administrator in "major" instances? The University of California, Merced (2007) distinguishes between "instructor-led" and "formal disciplinary" procedures for addressing different situations.

APPENDIX A

◇◇◇◇◇◇◇◇◇◇◇◇◇◇◇◇◇◇◇◇

Survey Instrument

① Your Background

I am a [☐ full-time ☐ part-time] employee.

Which division/school or program do you teach in? Check all that apply:

☐ Business

☐ Education

☐ Humanities

☐ Natural Sciences/Math

☐ Social Sciences

☐ Adult Education

☐ Music

☐ Seminary

☐ Nursing

☐ Library

☐ Other: _____

_____

_____

② Definition

How do you define "academic dishonesty"?

_____

_____

_____

_____

_____

_____

③ Communication

How do you inform your students about your policies regarding academic dishonesty? Check all that apply:

☐ I include a statement in the course syllabus.

☐ I hand out a written policy sometime during the course.

☐ I make a general announcement sometime during the course.

☐ I refer students to the university catalog or student handbook.

☐ I refer students to a written department/program policy.

☐ Other (please specify): _____

_____

④ Experiences

What forms of academic dishonesty have you encountered; how often?	Rarely > Occasionally > Frequently					
	0	1	2	3	4	5
☐ Cheating on an in-class exam	☐	☐	☐	☐	☐	☐
☐ Cheating on a take-home exam	☐	☐	☐	☐	☐	☐
☐ Copying ungraded assignments	☐	☐	☐	☐	☐	☐
☐ Copying graded assignments	☐	☐	☐	☐	☐	☐
☐ Plagiarism of less than 1 page	☐	☐	☐	☐	☐	☐
☐ Plagiarism of 1-5 pages	☐	☐	☐	☐	☐	☐
☐ Plagiarism of an entire term paper	☐	☐	☐	☐	☐	☐

☐ Other (please specify): _____

_____

_____

_____

⑤ Sanctions

How was the offender penalized in each case?

Cheating on an in-class exam

_____

Cheating on a take-home exam

_____

Copying ungraded assignments

_____

Copying graded assignments

_____

Plagiarism of less than 1 page

_____

Plagiarism of 1-5 pages

_____

Plagiarism of an entire term paper

_____

Other:

_____

⑥ Magnitude

	Less Serious > More Serious					
	0	1	2	3	4	5

How would you rate the seriousness of each of these types of academic dishonesty?

During a test...

	0	1	2	3	4	5
Talking	☐	☐	☐	☐	☐	☐
Glancing at another student's test	☐	☐	☐	☐	☐	☐
Looking at another student's test	☐	☐	☐	☐	☐	☐
Looking at notes or books	☐	☐	☐	☐	☐	☐
Consulting with another student on a take-home test	☐	☐	☐	☐	☐	☐
Having access to earlier editions of the test	☐	☐	☐	☐	☐	☐

Completing a homework assignment...

	0	1	2	3	4	5
Copying an ungraded assignment	☐	☐	☐	☐	☐	☐
Copying a graded assignment	☐	☐	☐	☐	☐	☐
Consulting with another student	☐	☐	☐	☐	☐	☐
Reading the "Cliff's Notes" edition rather than the assigned edition	☐	☐	☐	☐	☐	☐

Completing a paper or project...

	0	1	2	3	4	5
Failing to cite one or two short quotes	☐	☐	☐	☐	☐	☐
Failing to cite a longer quote	☐	☐	☐	☐	☐	☐
Failing to cite many quotes	☐	☐	☐	☐	☐	☐
Improperly citing sources (*e.g.*, omitting page numbers or authors)	☐	☐	☐	☐	☐	☐
Not conforming to the assigned style sheet	☐	☐	☐	☐	☐	☐
Using the same paper or project for assignments in different classes	☐	☐	☐	☐	☐	☐
Buying or downloading a term paper	☐	☐	☐	☐	☐	☐

What penalties would you suggest for...

The "more serious" instances (4 & 5 above): _____

_____

The "serious" instances (2 & 3 above): _____

_____

The "less serious" instances (0 & 1 above): _____

_____

◇◇◇◇◇◇◇◇◇◇◇◇◇◇◇◇◇

Survey Results

Table B1: Frequency of Academic Dishonesty Encountered[1]

Types of Academic Dishonesty Encountered	Frequency Encountered			
	Never/NA	Rarely	Occasionally	Frequently
Cheating on an in-class exam	24	22	6	0
Cheating on a take-home exam	34	9	9	0
Copying ungraded assignments	29	11	11	1
Copying graded assignments	26	12	14	0
Plagiarism of less than 1 page	14	11	20	7
Plagiarism of 1–5 pages	26	18	7	1
Plagiarism of entire term paper	40	8	4	0
Other	46	3	0	0

[1] Source: Survey of 52 North Park faculty members

Table B2: Sanctions Imposed or Suggested by Type of Misconduct[1]

Types of Academic Dishonesty Encountered	Sanctions Imposed or Suggested	
Cheating on an in-class or take-home exam	► Failed exam (14) ► Failed exam or course (5) ► Gave warning (2) ► Expelled for stealing tests (2) ► "It depends" (1) ► Met with student (1)	► Gave alternative exam (1) ► Retested student (1) ► Moved student (1) ► Lowered grade (1) ► Took test away & graded part done (1) ► Implemented new procedures (1)
Copying ungraded assignments	► Failed assignment (no credit given) (8) ► Redid assignment (2)	► Gave warning (6) ► Encouraged student to use own skills (2)

Table B2: Sanctions Imposed or Suggested by Type of Misconduct[1]

Types of Academic Dishonesty Encountered	Sanctions Imposed or Suggested	
Copying graded assignments	► Failed assignment (10) ► Lowered grade (3) ► Talked with student (3)	► Gave warning (1) ► Clarified expectations about group work (1)
Plagiarism of less than 1 page	► Revised/redid assignment (8) ► Lowered grade (8) ► Failed assignment (6) ► Gave warning (3) ► Offered instruction on avoiding plagiarism in the future (1)	► Redid with lower grade (2) ► Confronted student (1) ► Failed course (1) ► Failed course or assignment (1) ► Dismissed from program (1)
Plagiarism of 1-5 pages	► Failed assignment (9) ► Redid with lower grade (4) ► Redid assignment (4) ► Failed course (3)	► Redid or failed course (1) ► Failed assignment/course (1) ► Dismissed from program (1) ► "It depends" (1)
Plagiarism of entire term paper	► Failed course (4) ► Failed assignment or course (depending) (1) ► Failed assignment (2)	► Failed course or redid assignment (depending) (1) ► Administration allowed student to rewrite (1)
Other	► Dismissed from school (1) ► Failed assignment (1)	► Redid assignment (1)

[1] Source: Survey of 52 North Park faculty members
N.B. Many instructors stated that repeat offenders would receive an F in the course.

Table B3: Magnitude of Seriousness of Academic Dishonesty[1]

Types of Academic Dishonesty Encountered	Magnitude of Seriousness			
	Less Serious	Serious	More Serious	n/a
During a test...				
Talking	16	23	12	1
Glancing at another student's test	10	20	22	0
Looking at another student's test	1	11	40	0
Looking at notes or books	1	10	41	0
Consulting with another student on a take-home test	13	15	23	1
Having access to earlier editions of the test	9	12	29	2
Completing homework...				
Copying an ungraded assignment	8	25	18	1
Copying a graded assignment	1	15	35	1
Consulting with another student	28	19	3	2

Table B3: Magnitude of Seriousness of Academic Dishonesty[1]

Types of Academic Dishonesty Encountered	Magnitude of Seriousness			
	Less Serious	Serious	More Serious	n/a
Reading the "Cliff's Notes" edition rather than the assigned edition	15	25	6	6
Completing a paper or project...				
Failing to cite one or two short quotes	17	23	11	1
Failing to cite a longer quote	3	24	24	1
Failing to cite many quotes	2	11	38	1
Improperly citing sources	18	20	13	1
Not conforming to the assigned style sheet	19	27	4	1
Using the same paper or project for different classes	11	19	19	2
Buying a term paper	0	0	50	0

[1] Source: Survey of 52 North Park faculty members

Table B4: Sanctions Suggested by Degree of Seriousness[1]

Magnitude of Academic Dishonesty	Sanctions Suggested	
More serious	➤ Fail course (16) ➤ Fail course or assignment (4) ➤ Fail assignment/no credit (18) ➤ Redo with lower grade (2) ➤ Expel (1)	➤ Redo assignment (2) ➤ Lower grade (3) ➤ Lower grade or no credit (1) ➤ Academic review/suspend (2) ➤ Expel if repeated (2)
Serious	➤ Fail course (2) ➤ Fail course or assignment (3) ➤ Fail assignment/no credit (9) ➤ Redo with lower grade (2) ➤ Fail or redo w/lower grade (1) ➤ Warning (9)	➤ Redo assignment (8) ➤ Lower grade (11) ➤ Fail assignment/ lower grade (1) ➤ Academic review/suspend (1) ➤ From a warning to an F (1)
Less serious	➤ Fail assignment/no credit (3) ➤ Lower grade (6) ➤ Redo assignment (4) ➤ Redo with lower grade (1)	➤ Warning (24) ➤ Nothing (5) ➤ Academic review (1)

[1] Source: Survey of 52 North Park faculty members

◇◇◇◇◇◇◇◇◇◇◇◇◇◇◇◇

Sample Statement on Academic Dishonesty

The following is a reproduction of the "Statement Concerning Academic Dishonesty" section of North Park University's 1997 Student Handbook and Daily Planner:[1]

Academic dishonesty runs counter to the goals and ideals of every educational institution, will not be tolerated at North Park university, and may result in dismissal. Appropriate designated authorities within the University will judge cases of alleged academic dishonesty according to the principles, policies, and procedures outlined in the Student and Faculty Handbooks.

Categories and Definitions Explaining What Constitutes Academic Dishonesty

CHEATING ON QUIZZES, TESTS, AND/OR EXAMINATIONS

Cheating is defined as an individual or group activity for the purpose of dishonestly obtaining and/or distributing testable information prior to, during, or after an examination. Examples of dishonest activities include, but are not limited to, the following:

◆ Looking at an examination paper or answer sheet of another student.
◆ Obtaining unauthorized information about the test.prior to administration of the test.

---

[1] As seen on pages 52–55 of the *Handbook*; Reproduced by permission.

- Possessing or distributing a test prior to its administration, without the express permission of the instructor.
- Using any unauthorized materials or equipment during an examination.
- Cooperating or aiding in any of the above.

PLAGIARISM

Plagiarism is defined as any attempt to represent the words or ideas of another (whether published or unpublished) as one's own. Examples of such activities include, but are not limited to, the following:

- Using the words of a published source in a written exercise without appropriate documentation.
- Presenting as one's own the original concepts, ideas, and/or arguments of another source.
- Presenting as one's own another's computer programs, scientific research, or artistic creations without properly acknowledging the source of such material.
- Any student(s) knowingly violating this policy will be subject to the policy on academic dishonesty stated below.

ALTERATION OF ACADEMIC RECORDS

Examples include, but are not limited to, the following:

- Changing documentation in the Records Office (by computer or any other means).
- Changing entries in an instructor's grade book.
- Changing an answer to an already-graded academic exercise in order to falsely negotiate for a higher grade.

SABOTAGE

Examples include, but are not limited to, the following:

- Stealing, destroying, or altering another's academic work (such as an artwork, a computer program, a lab experiment/report, a paper).
- Hiding, misshelving, mutilating, or otherwise abusing library materials to keep others from using them.

SUBSTITUTION

Substitution is defined as using a proxy or acting as a proxy in an academic exercise. Examples include, but are not limited to, the following:

◆ Taking an examination for another student.

◆ Doing homework assignments for another student.

Judicial Procedures to be Followed in Cases of Academic Dishonesty

The instructor, on becoming aware of a possible instance of academic dishonesty, shall:

◆ Notify the student of the charge against him or her.

◆ Determine whether the student is guilty of an infraction; if so, report findings and a proposed penalty to the dean of the University Faculty and to the student.

A student who has knowledge of academic dishonesty should report this knowledge to the instructor of the course and to the dean of the University Faculty.

The dean of the University Faculty, on receipt of the instructor's report, shall:

◆ Inform the student and receive his or her response.

◆ Evaluate the instructor's report; upon concurrence in the finding, determine the appropriate penalty taking into consideration the instructor's recommendations.

◆ Convene a meeting with the instructor and student, at which time the student shall be informed of the decision and his or her right to appeal.

◆ Inform the dean of Student Life.

◆ Keep appropriate records of each case to its completion.

The student may:

◆ Accept the decision and the penalty.

◆ Appeal the decision to the Academic Judicial Committee (the appeal must come within two weeks of notice of the decision).

Upon timely appeal, the Academic Judicial Committee shall be convened at a time determined by the dean of the University Faculty. The committee shall consist of three faculty members appointed by the Dean. At least one of these faculty members shall be from among faculty not currently teaching the charged student. At least one of these faculty members shall be from the division offering the course. The committee shall also include three student members nominated (together with two alternates) by the Student Association Nominating Committee and confirmed by the Student Senate. A seventh member of the Committee shall be the vice chair of the faculty, who shall provide and cast a vote in the event of a tie. The charged student has the right to challenge one student and one faculty member on the committee; this challenge must be exercised within twenty-four hours of the student's receipt of the list of the members on his/her committee. The student may have one advisor (student or faculty) of his/her choosing to sit with them throughout the hearing. Witnesses will not be present for the entire hearing. The hearing will not be public.

The Academic Judicial Committee may:

◆ Reverse the finding and dismiss the case.

◆ Confirm the finding and the penalty imposed.

◆ Confirm the finding and alter the penalty.

The student may:

◆ Accept the decision of the Academic Judicial Committee.

◆ Appeal to the president of the University for clemency.

The decision of the president shall be final.

One or more of the following penalties may be imposed once academic dishonesty has been confirmed (previous infractions will be considered in the imposition of such penalties):

◆ A record of the infraction on the student's permanent record card.

◆ A failing grade on the examination, paper, or project.

◆ A failing grade in the course.

◆ Suspension from the University for an appropriate period.

◆ Expulsion from the University.

◆ Exclusion from participation in the athletic, musical, and other extra-curricular programs of the University.

◇◇◇◇◇◇◇◇◇◇◇◇◇◇◇◇

Ethics Policy

The following is a reproduction of the "Ethics Policy" portion of a syllabus for a history course taught by Dr. David Koeller. This portion was chosen because it articulates the professor's policy on academic honesty in a clear, concise, and thorough manner; as such, it may serve as a model for developing or revising syllabus statements on academic honesty.[2]

Classroom Behavior

North Park University is a Christian liberal arts university. As such, we expect our students and faculty to conduct themselves with honesty and integrity. Therefore, each student is expected to uphold high ethical standards inside and outside the classroom. The classroom should be an environment for learning; behavior which is disruptive, which belittles another, or which discourages others from achieving their academic goals has no place in this classroom.

Academic Misconduct

When you turn in an assignment and take credit for it, it must be your own work. If it is not, you have committed academic misconduct.

---

[2] As seen on pages 3-4, drafted by David Koeller, Professor of History at North Park University. Reproduced by permission.

PLAGIARISM

Plagiarism is representing the work of someone else as your own. Most commonly this occurs by copying from a textbook or other source and failing to give proper credit to the author. You may avoid this problem by always using quotation marks whenever you use someone else's exact words and by always giving references whenever you quote from or paraphrase another author.

CHEATING

If you give or receive unauthorized aid while completing any of the requirements for this course, you have cheated. Giving answers during an exam, writing a paper for another student, or copying another student's work are all forms of cheating. Assistance from the writing lab, talking with a professor or fellow student, or forming a study group before an exam are all acceptable forms of aid.

Penalties

The penalties for violation of this ethics policy will range, at the discretion of the instructor, from redoing assignments, to failing the course, to appearing before the dean.

◇◇◇◇◇◇◇◇◇◇◇◇◇◇◇◇◇◇

Sample Institutional Policies

Colleges and universities develop comprehensive policies and procedures to deal with cases of academic misconduct. These guidelines are meant to fulfill many roles: they define the scope of inappropriate behaviors; they provide steps (*i.e.*, due process) for students and faculty to follow when an instance of misconduct is suspected; and they outline the penalties associated with various infractions. Because most policies and procedures are long, complex, and unique to each institution's circumstances, it would not be practical to offer a "model policy." Instead, I am including a few on-line resources to be used as examples of comprehensive policies and procedures. The resources were chosen on the basis of institutional variety (*i.e.*, public and private, as well as small and large, colleges and universities). Each policy offers an institutional vision of academic integrity, clear definitions, student responsibilities, actions taken by faculty and deans, an overview of due process, hearings, appeals, and sanctions for first time and repeat offenders. An institution's administration must consult with legal consul as it works to develop and refine its own comprehensive policy and set of procedures.

Source	Web Site
Beloit College	www.beloit.edu/~stuaff/Handbook/#dishonesty
De Pauw University	www.depauw.edu/univ/handbooks/dpuhandbookprint.asp?indexnum=101
Penn State University	www.psu.edu/oue/aappm/G-9.html
Tacoma Community College	www.tacomacc.edu/resourcesforstudents/studentpolicies/administrativeprocedureforacademicdishonesty.aspx
University of Iowa	www.clas.uiowa.edu/students/academic_handbook/ix.shtml

References

Aaron, R. 1992. Student academic dishonesty: Are collegiate institutions addressing the issue? *NASPA Journal.* 29: 107–113.

Aaron, R. and R. Georgia. 1994. Administrator perceptions of student academic dishonesty in collegiate institutions. *NASPA Journal.* 31: 83–91.

Academic Senate for California Community Colleges. 1994. *Faculty Ethics: Expanding the AAUP Ethics Statement.* ERIC Document Reproduction Service No. ED 369-442. Available at: <http://eric.ed.gov/ERICWebPortal/contentdelivery/servlet/ERICServlet?accno=ED 369442>.

Alschuler, A. and G. Blimling. 1995. Curbing epidemic cheating through systemic change. *College Teaching.* 43: 123–126.

Applebome, P. 1997. On the Internet, term papers are hot items. *The New York Times.* 1 (June 8).

Arizona State University. 2007. *Student Academic Integrity Policy (Web page).* Retrieved May 12 from: <www.asu.edu/studentaffairs/studentlife/judicial/academic_integrity.htm>.

Beemsterboer, P., J. Odom, T. Pate, and N. K. Haden. 2000. Issues of academic integrity in U.S. dental schools. *Journal of Dental Education.* 12: 833–838.

Bell, D. 2005. Resolving academic dishonesty through facilitated discussion. *Academic Leader.* 21: 3–8.

Birchard, K. 2006. Cheating is rampant in Canadian colleges. *The Chronicle of Higher Education.* 53(8): A53. Available at: <http://chronicle.com/weekly/v53/i08/08a05302.htm>.

Blaine v. Savannah Country Day School, Ga. App. 491 S.E. 2D 446 (1997).

Board of Curators of University of Missouri v. Horowitz, 435 U.S. 78 (1978).

Boehm v. University of Pennsylvania School of Veterinary Medicine, 573 A. 2d. 575 (Pa. Super. 1990).

Bowers, W. J. 1964. *Student dishonesty and its control in college.* New York: Bureau of Applied Social Research, Columbia University.

California State University, Fullerton. 2003. Dean of Students Office. In *Student Handbook and Planner 2006–2007,* edited by L. Martin. Available at: <www.fullerton.edu/handbook/resources/dos.htm>.

Carr v. St. John's University, New York, 231 N.Y.S. 2d 410 (N.Y. App. Div. 1962).

CBC News. 2006. Forged transcripts plague Vancouver college. *CBC.ca*. Available at: <www.cbc.ca/canada/british-columbia/story/2006/09/07/bc-transcripts.html>.

Cheathouse 2007. *Home page*. Available at: <www.cheathouse.com>.

Clayton v. Trustees of Princeton University, 519 F. Supp. 802 (D. N.J. 1981).

Corcoran, K. and J. Rotter. 1987. Morality-conscience guilt scale as a predictor of ethical behavior in a cheating situation among college females. *Journal of General Psychology*. 114: 117–123.

Coscio v. Medical College of Wisconsin, Inc., 407 N.W. 2d 302 (Wis. App. 1987).

Croucher, J. 1994. The complete guide to exam cheating. *New Scientist*. 142: 48–49.

Dames, M. 2006. Plagiarism: The new 'piracy.' *Information Today*. 23: 21–22.

Dannells, M. 1997. From discipline to development. *ASHE-ERIC Pub. [Vol. 25 (2)]*. Washington, D.C.: George Washington University.

Davis, B. G. 1993. *Tools for Teaching*. San Francisco, CA: Jossey-Bass.

Davis, S. 1993. Cheating in college is for a career: Academic dishonesty in the 1990s. Paper presented at the 39th Meeting of the Southeastern Psychological Association, Atlanta, GA.

DeFrancesco, L. 2002. Graduate admissions crackdown. *The Scientist*. 3(1). Available at: <www.the-scientist.com/article/display/20694/>.

Deal, W. 1984. Cheating. *Journal of Chemical Education*. 61: 797.

Dehaan v. Brandeis University, 150 F. Supp. 626 (D. Mass. 1957).

Desruisseaux, P. 1996. A record number of foreign students enrolled at U.S. colleges last year. *The Chronicle of Higher Education*. 43(15): A64–67.

Dickenson, H. 1945. Identical errors and deception. *Journal of Educational Research*. 38: 534–542.

District Court, Kansas City, MO. 1968. *General Order on Judicial standards of procedure and substance in review of student discipline in tax-supported institutions of higher education*, 45 F.R.D. 133, 136 (W.D. Mo. 1968).

Dixon v. Alabama State Board of Education, 294 F.2d 150, 158 (5th Cir. 1961).

Dowd, S. 1992. *Academic Integrity: A Review and Case Study*. ERIC Document Reproduction Service No. ED 349-060. Available at: <http://eric.ed.gov/ERICWebPortal/content delivery/servlet/ERICServlet?accno=ED349060>.

Duke University. 2007a. *Faculty/Instructors of Undergraduates (Web page)*. Retrieved May 12 from: <http://judicial.studentaffairs.duke.edu/audiencenav/faculty_instructors.html>.

———. 2007b. *Academic Integrity Council (Home page)*. Retrieved May 12 from: <www.integrity.duke.edu>.

Dwyer, D. and J. Hecht. 1994. *Cheating Detection: Statistical, Legal, and Policy Implications*. ERIC Document Reproduction Service No. ED 382-066. Available at: <http://eric.ed.gov/ERICWebPortal/contentdelivery/servlet/ERICServlet?accno=ED382066>.

———. 1996. Using statistics to catch cheaters: methodological and legal issues for student personnel administrators. *NASPA Journal*. 33: 125–135.

Eisenberger, R. and D. H. Shank. 1985. Personal work ethic and effort training affect cheating. *Journal of Personality and Social Psychology*. 49: 520–528.

Empire State College. 2004. *Academic Honesty Policy and Procedures (Web page)*. Available at: <www.esc.edu/ESConline/ESCdocuments/policies.nsf/88be7f1cdc8900eb85256c1d0051 89dd/3b314e5b28c9195185256eb40061ebe1?OpenDocument>.

Esteban v. Central Missouri State College, 227 F. Supp. 649 (W.D. Mo. 1967).

Fairclough, G. 1995. Wrong answer. *Far Eastern Economic Review*. 158: 43.

Fanning, P. 1992. Countering language plagiarism: A materials approach. *Crosscurrents*. 19: 167–173.

Ferguson, W. and J. York. 2003. Through UT's back door. *The Daily Texan Online*. September 22. Available at: <http://media.www.dailytexanonline.com/media/storage/paper410/news/2003/09/22/TopStories/Through.Uts.Back.Door-471683.shtml>.

Fishbein, L. 1994. We can curb college cheating. *Education Digest.* 59: 58–61.

Florida State University. 2004. ENC 1102 Plagiarism exercise (Web page). In *First-Year Composition Teachers' Guide.* Available at: <http://english3.fsu.edu/writing/?q=node/283>.

Foster, A. 2003. On the Web, it's easy to earn straight A's. *The Chronicle of Higher Education.* 49(22). Available at: <http://chronicle.com/weekly/v49/i22/22a02501.htm>.

Frary, R. and T. N. Tideman. 1997. Comparison of two indices of answer copying and development of a spliced index. *Educational and Psychological Measurement.* 57: 20–32.

Gaspar v. Bruton, 513 F.2d 843 (10th Cir. 1975).

George Washington University. 2005. *Code of Academic Integrity.* Available at: <www.gwu.edu/~ntegrity/code.html>.

———. 2007. *First-Year Writing.* Retrieved from: <www.gwu.edu/~uwp/fyw/fyw-about.htm>.

Georgia College and State University. 2007. Student academic dishonesty. In *Academic Policies and Regulations.* Retrieved May 12 from: <http://catalog.gcsu.edu/4DCGI/Catalog/under/SubHeadingDetail/107>.

Goss v. Lopez, 419 U.S. 565 (1975).

Greenhill v. Bailey, 519 F.2d 5 (8th Cir. 1975).

Guiliano, E. 2000. Deterring plagiarism in the age of the internet. *Inquiry.* 5: 22–31.

Halfond, J. 1991. Academic dishonesty in the business school: A case study. *Business and Professional Ethics Journal.* 10: 101–106.

Hansen, B. 2003. Combating plagiarism. *CQ (Congressional Quarterly) Researcher.* 13: 775–791.

Hard, S., J. Conway, and A. Moran. 2006. Faculty and college student beliefs about the frequency of student academic misconduct. *Journal of Higher Education.* 77: 1058–1080.

Harpp, D. 1991. Big prof is watching you. *Discover.* 12: 12–3.

Hatch, G. 1992. The crime of plagiarism: A critique of literary property law. Paper presented at the 43rd Conference on College Composition and Communication, Cincinnati, OH.

Havers, F. 1996. Testing fraud exposed: GRE, GMAT, TOEFL cheating scam uncovered. *Yale Herald.* October 31. Available at: <www.yaleherald.com/archive/xxii/10.31.96/news/gre.html>.

Hoekema, D. 1994. *Campus Rules and Moral Community: In Place of In Loco Parentis.* Lanham, MD: Rowman and Littlefield.

Hollinger, R. and L. Lanza-Kaduce. 1996. Academic dishonesty and the perceived effectiveness of countermeasures: An empirical survey of cheating at a major public university. *NASPA Journal.* 33: 292–306.

Jaska v. Regents of University of Michigan, 597 F. Supp. 1245 (D. C. Mich. 1984).

Jendrek, M. 1989. Faculty reactions to academic dishonesty. *Journal of College Student Development.* 30: 401–406.

———. 1992. Students' reactions to academic dishonesty. *Journal of College Student Development.* 33: 260–273.

Julliard, K. 1994. Perceptions of plagiarism in the use of other authors' language. *Family Medicine.* 26: 356–360.

Kaplin, W. and B. Lee. 1995. *The Law of Higher Education.* San Francisco: Jossey-Bass.

Kibler, W. 1993a. Academic dishonesty: A student development dilemma. *NASPA Journal.* 30: 252–267.

———. 1993b. A framework for addressing academic dishonesty from a student development perspective. *NASPA Journal.* 31: 8–18.

———. 1994. Addressing academic dishonesty: What are institutions of higher education doing and not doing? *NASPA Journal.* 31: 92–101.

Koeller, D. 2006. *Course syllabus for HIST 3450 Twentieth Century Germany.* Available at: <www.thenagain.info/Classes/Basics/Syllabus.GerS06.doc>.

Landau, J., P. Druen, and J. Arcuri. 2002. Methods for helping students avoid plagiarism. *Teaching of Psychology*. 29: 112–115.

Leeds, J. 1992. The course syllabus seen by the undergraduate student. Paper presented at the 100th Meeting of the American Psychological Association, Washington, D.C.

Lefkos, P. 2006. Students faking documents to gain admission. *The Voice*. 11(October 5). Available at: <www.langara.bc.ca/voice/documents/01a11_000.pdf>.

Lipson, A. and N. McGavern. 1993. Undergraduate academic dishonesty at MIT. Paper presented at the 33rd Forum of the Association for Institutional Research, Chicago, IL.

Maddox, J. 1995. Plagiarism is worse than theft. *Nature*. 376: 721.

Malesic, J. 2005. How dumb do they think we are? *The Chronicle of Higher Education*. 53(17): C3. Available at: <http://chronicle.com/weekly/v53/i17/17c00201.htm>.

Mangan, K. S. 1997. Plagiarism case at St. Thomas U. Law School angers professors. *The Chronicle of Higher Education*. 43(24): A11. Available at: <http://chronicle.com/che-data/articles.dir/art-43.dir/issue-24.dir/24a01102.htm>.

———. 2002a. UCLA heightens scrutiny of foreign applicants. *The Chronicle of Higher Education*. 49(5). Available at: <http://chronicle.com/weekly/v49/i05/05a05801.htm>.

———. 2002b. The fine art of fighting fakery. *The Chronicle of Higher Education*. 49(10). Available at: <http://chronicle.com/weekly/v49/i10/10a03901.htm>.

Maramark, S. and M. Maline. 1993. *Academic Dishonesty Among College Students*. Washington: U. S. Department of Education, Office of Educational Research and Improvement.

May, K. and B. Loyd. 1993. Academic dishonesty: The honor system and students' attitudes. *Journal of College Students Development*. 34: 125–129.

McCabe, D. 2005. It takes a village: Academic dishonesty and educational opportunity. *Liberal Education*. 91: 26–31.

McCabe, D. and G. Pavela. 2005. New honor codes for a new generation. *Inside Higher Ed*. March 11. Available at: <www.insidehighered.com/views/2005/03/14/pavela1>.

McCabe, D. and L. Trevino. 1993. Academic dishonesty: Honor codes and other contextual influences. *Journal of Higher Education*. 64: 522–538.

———. 1996. What we know about cheating in college. *Change*. 28: 28–33.

McCabe, D. and W. J. Bowers. 1996. The relationship between student cheating and college fraternity or sorority membership. *NASPA Journal*. 33: 280–291.

McCabe, D., K. Butterfield, and L. Trevino. 2006. Academic dishonesty in graduate business programs: Prevalence, causes, and proposed action. *Academy of Management Learning and Education*. 5: 294–306.

McCollum, K. 1996. Term-paper Web site has professors worried about plagiarism. *The Chronicle of Higher Education*. 42(47): A28. Available at: <http://chronicle.com/che-data/articles.dir/art-42.dir/issue-47.dir/47a02801.htm>.

———. 1997. On-line sale of essays may help students get into colleges. *The Chronicle of Higher Education*. 43(25): A25–26.

McQuade, S. C. 2007. We must educate young people about cybercrime before they start college. *The Chronicle of Higher Education*. 53(18): B29. Available at: <http://chronicle.com/weekly/v53/i18/18b02901.htm>.

Melvin v. Union College. 600 N.Y.S.2d 141 (N.Y. App. Div. 1993).

Michigan Technological University. 2006. *Academic Integrity Policy*. Available at: <www.studentaffairs.mtu.edu/dean/judicial/policies/academic_integrity.html>.

Milam, S. and R. Marshall. 1987. Impact of Regents of the University of Michigan v. Ewing on academic dismissals from graduate and professional schools. Journal of College and University Law. 13(4): 335–352.

Mobiledia Corp. 2005. Students using cell phones for high-tech cheating. *Mobiledia.com*. March 12. Available at: <www.mobiledia.com/news/26810.html>.

Narita, E. 2004. Cell phone cheating not big OSU problem. *The Lantern*. 1 (September 29).

National Association of Student Personnel Administrators. 1993. *Student Rights and Freedoms*. Joint Statement on Rights and Freedoms of Students. ERIC Document Reproduction Service No. ED355880. Available at: <http://eric.ed.gov/ERICWebPortal/contentdelivery/servlet/ERICServlet?accno=ED355880>.

Nelson, H. 1995. The Academic Dishonesty Question: A Guide to an Answer through Education, Prevention, Adjudication, and Obligation. Available at: <http://hep.ucsb.edu/people/hnn/conduct/disq.html>.

North Park University. 1997. *Student Handbook and Daily Planner*. Chicago, IL.

Northwestern University. 2006. *Definitions of Academic Violations (Web page)*. Available at: <www.northwestern.edu/uacc/defines.html>.

Oakton Community College. 1997. *Student Handbook*. Des Plaines, IL.

Oklahoma State University. 2006. *New Student Orientation Welcome Week (Web page)*. Available at: <www.gradcollege.okstate.edu/events/current/welcomeweek.html>.

Other People's Papers. 2007. *Home page*. Retrieved May 12 from: <www.OPPapers.com>.

Pancrazio, S. and G. Aloia. 1992. Evaluating university policies on plagiarism and other forms of research. *North Central Association Quarterly*. 67: 335–342.

Payne, S. and K. Nantz. 1994. Social accounts and metaphors about cheating. *College Teaching*. 42: 90–96.

Pellegrino, E. 1991. In search of integrity. *Journal of the American Medical Association*. 266: 2452.

Psychology Today (Staff Writers). Your cheatin' heart. 1992. *Psychology Today*. 25: 9. Available at: <www.psychologytoday.com/articles/pto-19921101-000003.html>.

Regents of University of Michigan v. Ewing, 106 S. Ct. 507 (1985).

Reilly v. Daly, 666 N. E. 2d 439 (C.A. Indiana 1996).

Renard, L. 2000. Cut-and-paste 101: Plagiarism and the Net. *Educational Leadership*. 57: 38–42.

Richland Community College. 2007. *Application for Admission*. Available at: <www.illinois mentor.org/Applications/Richland_Community_College/apply.html?application_id=3447>.

Risacher, J. and W. Slonaker. 1996. Academic misconduct: NASPA institutional members' views and a pragmatic model policy. *NASPA Journal*. 33: 105–124.

Robinson, J. 1992. International students and American university culture: Adjustment issues. Paper presented at the Washington Area Teachers of English to Speakers of Other Languages Annual Convention, Arlington, VA.

Rogers, A. 1996. For $6,000, you get a pencil with the answers included: Federal agents break up a cheating ring charged with beating graduate-school entrance exams. *Newsweek*. November 11: 69.

Roig, M. 1997. Can undergraduate students determine whether text has been plagiarized? *Psychological Record*. 47: 113–122.

Roig, M. and L. de Tommaso. 1995. Are college cheating and plagiarism related to academic procrastination? *Psychological Reports*. 76: 763–768.

Roig, M. and M. Caso. 2005. Lying and cheating: Fraudulent excuse making, cheating, and plagiarism. *Journal of Psychology*. 139: 485–494.

Ross, K. 2005. Academic dishonesty and the internet. *Communications of the ACM (Association for Computing Machinery)*. 48: 29–31.

Rozance, C. 1991. Cheating in medical schools: Implications for students and patients. *Journal of the American Medical Association*. 266: 2453.

School Sucks. 2007. *Home page*. Retrieved May 12 from: <www.schoolsucks.com>.

Selingo, J. 2004. The cheating culture. *Prism: American Society for Engineering Education*. 14(1). Available at: <www.prism-magazine.org/sept04/feature_cheating.htm>.

Shuffer v. Board of Trustees of the California State University and Colleges, 67 Cal. App. 3d 208 (136 Cal. Rptr. 527, 1977).

Smith, B. 2007. *Dealing with the Problem of Plagiarism (Web page).* Available at: <http://men dota.english.wisc.edu/~WAC/page.jsp?id=106&c_type=category&c_id=44>.

Smith, M., M. Dupre, and D. Mackey. 2005. Deterring research paper plagiarism with technology: Establishing a department-level electronic research paper database with e-mail. *Journal of Criminal Justice Education.* 16: 193–204.

Soglin v. Kauffman, 418 F.2d 163 (7th Cir. 1969).

Spiller, S. and D. Crown. 1995. Changes over time in academic dishonesty at the collegiate level. *Psychological Reports.* 76: 763–768.

Spuches, C. 2001. *A Course Syllabus Checklist (Web page).* State University of New York College of Environmental Science and Forestry. Available at: <www.esf.edu/iq/focus/syllabus.htm>.

State University of New York at Brockport. 2003. Policy on student academic dishonesty (Web page). In *2006–2007 Your Right to Know & Academic Policies Handbook,* Chapter 7. <www. brockport.edu/publications/yrtk/importantPolicies.html#Policy>.

State University of New York at Stony Brook. 2006. *Policies and Procedures Governing Undergraduate Student Academic Dishonesty (Web page).* Available at: <http://naples.cc. stonybrook.edu/CAS/ajc.nsf/pages/info>.

Sterngold, A. 2004. Confronting plagiarism: How conventional teaching invites cyber-cheating. *Change.* 36: 16–21.

Stevens, E. 1996. Informal resolution of academic misconduct cases: A due process paradigm. *College Teaching.* 44: 140–144.

Stevens, G. and F. Stevens. 1987. Ethical inclinations of tomorrow's managers revisited. *Journal of Education for Business.* 63: 24–29.

Strosnider, K. 1996. Man charged with putting answers to tests on pencils. *The Chronicle of Higher Education.* 43(11): A38. Available at: <http://chronicle.com/che-data/articles.dir/ art-43.dir/issue-11.dir/11a03801.htm>.

Susan M. v. New York Law School, 557 N.Y.S. 2d 297 (N.Y. 1990).

Sutton, E.M. and M. Huba. 1995. Undergraduate perceptions of academic dishonesty as a function of ethnicity and religious participation. *NASPA Journal.* 33: 19–34.

Swem, L. 1987. Due process rights in student disciplinary matters. *Journal of College and University Law.* 14(2): 359–382.

Swidryk v. Saint Michael's Medical Center, 493 A. 2d 641 (N. J. Super L. 1985).

Syracuse University. 2006a. *Academic Integrity Office (Web page).* Available at: <http://provost. syr.edu/academicintegrity_office.asp>.

———. 2006b. *Academic Integrity Policies and Procedures (Web page).* Available at: <http:// provost.syr.edu/SU_AI_Policies_Procedures.doc>.

Tedeschi v. Wagner College, 49 N.Y. 2d 652 (N.Y. 1980).

Tetzeli, R. 1991. Business students cheat most. *Fortune.* 124: 14.

The New Webster Encyclopedic Dictionary of the English Language. 1971. Chicago: Consolidated Book Publishers.

Thompson, L. and P. Williams. 1995. But I changed three words! Plagiarism in the ESL classroom. *The Clearing House.* 69: 27–29.

Thompson, M. 2005. Hidden in plain sight. *The Chronicle of Higher Education.* 52(15): B5. Available at: < http://chronicle.com/weekly/v52/i15/15b00501.htm>.

Trustees of Dartmouth College v. Woodward, 17 U.S. 518 (1819).

Turner, S. and P. Beemsterboer. 2003. Enhancing academic integrity: Formulating effective honor codes. *Journal of Dental Education.* 67: 1122–1129.

University of California, Berkeley. 2006. *Faculty and GSI Tips on Cheating in the Classroom (Web page).* Available at: <http://teaching.berkeley.edu/tipsoncheating.html>.

University of California, Merced. 2007. *Academic Honesty Policy.* <http://studentlife.ucmerced. edu/2.asp?uc=1&lvl2=121&lvl3=121&lvl4=123&contentid=171>.

University of Florida. 2007. *Reporting and Judicial Process for Academic Honesty Violations.* Retrieved May 12 from: <www.dso.ufl.edu/judicial/procedures/honestyprocess.php>.

University of Houston–Downtown. 2004. Academic honesty policy. In *Student Handbook 2004/2005.* Available at: <www.uhd.edu/campus/handbook0405/policies.htm>.

University of Maryland. 2005. *Code of Academic Integrity (Web page).* Available at: <www.studenthonorcouncil.umd.edu/code.html>.

University of Pennsylvania. 2006. *Orientation Events.* Available at: <www.upenn.edu/nso/2006/events/index.html>.

University of Rochester. 2004. *Academic Honesty at the College.* Available at: <www.rochester.edu/College/honesty/>.

University of Wisconsin–Eau Claire. 2006. *How to Be Successful Academically (Web page).* Available at: <www.uwec.edu/orientation/freshmen/successfulAcademically.htm>.

Van Sack, J. 2004. Cheating keeps getting easier: Students using cell phones to cheat on exams. *The Patriot Ledger.* June 14. Available at: <http://ledger.southofboston.com/articles/2004/06/14/news/news01.txt>.

Wagner, R. 1993. Medical student academic misconduct: Implications of recent case law and possible institutional responses. *Academic Medicine.* 68: 887–889.

Walcott, C. 2005. *Annual Report to the Board of Trustees, Cornell University.* Available at: <http://theuniversityfaculty.cornell.edu/dean/2005DeanTrusteeReport.pdf>.

Ward, D. 1986. Self-esteem and dishonest behavior revisited. *Journal of Social Psychology.* 126: 709–713.

Ward, D. and W. Beck. 1990. Gender and dishonesty. *Journal of Social Psychology.* 130: 333–339.

Washington State University. 2004. *Plagiarism Information for New Student Orientation.* Available at: <www.ip.wsu.edu/oiss/documents/students/Plagiarism-Intro.pdf>.

Weeks, K. 1996. Contract challenges and the student handbook. *Lex Collegii.* 19: 1–6.

———. 1997. Grade and test challenges. *Lex Collegii.* 21: 1–5.

Weeks, K. and D. Victor. 1982. Student handbooks: Rights and responsibilities. *Lex Collegii.* 6: 1–4.

Weeks, K. and M. Rice. 1986. Disciplinary dismissals and suspension of students and institutional policies. *Lex Collegii.* 9: 1–7.

Weideman v. SUNY College at Cortland, 592 N.Y.S. 2d 99 (N.Y. App. Div. 1992).

Weiser, B. 1997. Federal inquiry widens in testing scheme. *The New York Times.* August 13: B2.

Weiss, J., K. Gilbert, P. Giordano, and S. Davis. 1993. Academic dishonesty, type A behavior, and classroom orientation. *Bulletin of the Psychonomic Society.* 31: 101–102.

White, E. 1993. Too many campuses ignore student plagiarism. *The Chronicle of Higher Education.* 39(25): A44. Available at: <http://chronicle.com/che-data/articles.dir/articles-39.dir/issue-25.dir/25a04401.htm>.

Wilhoit, S. 1994. Helping students avoid plagiarism. *College Teaching.* 42: 161–164.

Wilmington College. 2007. *Academic Dishonesty.* Retrieved May 12 from: <www.wilmcoll.edu/studentlife/acaddishonesty.html>.

Witherspoon, A. 1995. This pen for hire: On grinding out papers for college students. *Harper's Magazine.* 290: 49–57.

Wolper, A. 1997. Cheating scandal aftermath. *Editor and Publisher.* 130: 16–19.

Woodruff v. Georgia State University, 251 Ga. 232, 234, 304 S.E. 2d 697 (1983).

Woody v. Burns, 188 So. 2d 56 (Fla. 1966).

Worcester Polytechnic Institute. 2006. *New Faculty Orientation 2006 (Web page).* Available at: <www.wpi.edu/Academics/CEDA/Services/nfo06.html>.

Yahn, L., and J. Jordon. 2007. *Is This Plagiarism (Web page)?* University of Connecticut. Retrieved from: <http://irc.uconn.edu/PlagiarismModule/IsThis_m.htm>.

Zumbrun v. University of Southern California, 101 Cal. Rptr. 499 (1972).